297

*The Old House Book of*

# Kitchens and Dining Rooms

**Other Titles in the Old House Books Series**

*The Old House Book of Bedrooms*
*The Old House Book of Living Rooms and Parlors*
*The Old House Book of Outdoor Living Spaces*
*The Brand New Old House Catalogue*

Forthcoming

*The Old House Book of Paints and Papers*

# *The Old House Book of*
# Kitchens and Dining Rooms

Lawrence Grow

WARNER BOOKS
A Warner Communications Company

A Main Street Press Book

Warner Books, Inc.
75 Rockefeller Plaza
New York, NY 10019

A Warner Communications Company

Printed in the United States of America

Designed by Frank Mahood

First printing: September 1981

10 9 8 7 6 5 4 3 2 1

Library of Congress Cataloging in Publication Data

THE OLD HOUSE BOOK OF KITCHENS AND DINING ROOMS

(THE OLD HOUSE BOOKS)

1. DWELLINGS—REMODELING. 2. KITCHENS—REMODELING. 3. DINING ROOMS—REMODELING. I. GROW, LAWRENCE. II. SERIES: OLD HOUSE BOOKS.
TH4816.042 643'.3 81-3036
ISBN 0-446-51233-8 AACR2
ISBN 0-446-97544-3 (pbk.)
ISBN 0-446-37099-1 (Can: pbk.)

# *Contents*

# Introduction

When remodeling is being considered, it is almost always the kitchen that is given priority. And for good reason. Cooking technology has changed drastically over the past 200 years and has rendered the typical room design of one period obsolete for another. Few housewives today are any more willing than women of the 19th century to forego improvements in food preparation and preservation. While other rooms—the living room, the bedroom, the dining room—have changed in style, the kitchen has been radically transformed in form and content. And change continues to come in this, the electronic age.

The kitchen may also show its age in other ways. Of all the rooms in the old house, the kitchen is the one that has been used the most. The early American kitchen was designed primarily for functional purposes, but it was not long before the space served more than as a center for preparing meals. In the typical 19th-century farmhouse, for example, the kitchen became the place where the family took most of its meals. It also became a center of evening activity in both rural and urban dwellings, a room in which to relax, the fireplace or cookstove providing welcome warmth in the cooler months of the year. During the day, nearly every member of the household was in and out of the room a dozen or so times, if only to use the "back" door located in or just off the kitchen.

In contrast, the dining room has been the least used of the rooms in the average house. Until the late 18th century, a separate space reserved only for meals was considered a luxury; not until the mid-1800s was a dining room commonly included in new house plans. By the 1850s nearly everyone wanted a dining room and all its basic appurtenances—matching table and chairs, sideboard, and china cabinet or cupboard—which symbolized bourgeois respectability. When colonial-period homes were remodeled in the 18th and 19th centuries with the addition of a separate kitchen wing or lean-to, one of the two original parlors, the "hall" in which cooking had originally taken place, was often given over to dining. In newly-built Victorian homes, the dining room was usually planned to connect directly with the kitchen and pantry on one side of the house. If the kitchen was located in the basement, a dumbwaiter was provided to carry dishes to

Opposite page: *"Evelyn, a little native maid," is the title of a 1909 photograph taken by Jessie Tarbox Beals. The scene graphically illustrates the reason why most old house kitchens meant to be used are never restored but, rather, are enthusiastically remodeled.*

the dining room overhead. The room became the social center of the dwelling in the 19th century, a place in which to entertain, to display one's degree of prosperity in china, silver, and glass, and to practice good manners. The extension dining table, introduced in the early 1800s, was the only "technical" innovation to affect the layout of the room. By being able to change the table size, the housewife could arrange the furnishings one way when entertaining and in another manner for everyday use. All other changes in the room's furnishings and decoration over time have been a matter of fashion.

Restoration is thus a goal more easily achieved in the dining room than in the kitchen. What *was* fashionable for dining sometime in the past may be perfectly workable for today. If the budget allows for antique furnishings, these can be obtained fairly easily over a period of time. Dining room furniture was often purchased in sets, and hundreds of thousands of these were manufactured in the 19th century. A more difficult problem is that of determining what style of decoration is appropriate, especially if the dining room was added to the house or extensively redecorated at a later time. In such cases, a style consistent with that found in the majority of the other rooms, whatever their age, is usually recommended.

No kitchen can be truly restored if it is to be used on a regular basis. This does not mean, however, that certain elements in the room's original make-up should not be recaptured. A fireplace closed up in the mid-19th century to make way for a cookstove might be reopened and used again—not for

*The oldest surviving kitchen in America is that found in the c. 1636 Fairbanks House, Dedham, Mass., now a museum. As furnished in this 1940 view, it lacks only a row of modern appliances along one wall to fit it out for daily use.*

*The dining room of the 1846 Bowen family house, "Roseland," in Woodstock, Conn., has changed little over the years. All of the Gothic Revival furniture is of a set made for the room in the 1840s. Steam heating and electricity were introduced without sacrificing any basic structural element.*

cooking but to restore the structural proportions of the room and to add period authenticity. On the other hand, it would be a mistake to construct a fireplace in a late-Victorian kitchen where only a chimney flue, used for venting the cookstove, now stands. It would be better to track down an antique stove or its modern equivalent for use as an auxilliary heating device. The type of furnishings used in old kitchens—freestanding cupboards, a worktable, a bench or settee—can also be put to effective new use, even in a kitchen containing the most modern appliances and storage spaces.

History will be your best guide in making decisions regarding the design and decoration of the old house dining room, and will help in deciding how to put together a kitchen that is both convenient to use and in character with the overall house style. If time has erased much of the visible evidence of what was in place, turn to the historical record. Hundreds of books were published during the 19th and early 20th centuries on housekeeping, and these often discuss the areas of the house in which food has been prepared and served. The historical record is less clear for the colonial period, but this has been pieced back together in the countless number of restored homes found in most areas of North America. A selection of this type of documentary information from present day and historical sources is presented in the following pages of *The Old House Book of Kitchens and Dining Rooms.* It constitutes an introduction to the subject, and, hopefully, a useful one.

# 1.
# *Cooking: From Fireplace to Electric Range*

For a century or more, popular artists have portrayed the kitchen hearth as the symbolic center of the American home. It is here that the home fires have most brightly glowed, that so much that has been traditionally valued—the fellowship of family and friends—has come into play. The typical scene, whether it be out of the nostalgic portfolio of Norman Rockwell or that of J. G. Brown, an earlier sentimentalist, includes children and often their mother, both sanctified as standard domestic fixtures—much like the vast array of rustic cooking utensils and devices that surround them. The kitchen is seen preeminently as the domain of the housewife, and the hearth as the altar at which she worships and from which good things flow to all who are deserving of them.

The Victorian sensibility which gave birth to this romanticization of past domesticity remains with us today, perhaps less cloying in its artistic representation, but nonetheless vital in expression. In this last quarter of the 20th century—and especially in popular

*This imaginative rendering of a peaceful colonial kitchen was painted in 1885 by Edward Hill. It presents a truer picture of the typical room of this period than the works of other Victorian romanticists, but the painter has taken some artistic license. Neither the Boston rocker near the windows nor the lantern above were available for household use until the 19th century.*

*"L-W Ranges Are Made To Please The Cook" was the headline which appeared with this artwork from a 1907 advertisement for a Lattimer-Williams Steel Leader Range. A coal-burning appliance similar to this model might have been installed in a kitchen as early as the 1880s and continued in use in many homes until the 1930s. The steel body was easier to clean than one of cast iron, and the oven, the manufacturer claimed, "will bake evenly and well."*

demonstrations at museum villages—there has even been a return to the primitive practice of cooking in the fireplace, a method gladly abandoned in most American homes in the mid-1800s when improved cooking technology began to render the fireplace obsolete. While this attempt at recovering a simpler past before mechanization, before the modernization of the kitchen, remains primarily academic, the seriousness with which it is pursued cannot be discounted. There is a strong desire to make of the ritual of preparing and serving food something more personally satisfying. Instant mixes and microwave technology help to satisfy hunger swiftly and effortlessly, but offer little to those who seek something more fulfilling. In her usual histrionic manner, Harriet Beecher Stowe said much the same during the 1860s when the fireplace was being abandoned for more advanced technology:

> Would our Revolutionary fathers have gone barefooted and bleeding over snows to defend air-tight stoves and cooking-ranges? It was the memory of the great open kitchen fire with its back-log and fore-stick of cord wood, its roaring, hilarious voice of invitation, its dancing tongue of flames, that called to them through the snows of that dreadful winter to keep up their courage, that made their hearts warm and bright with a thousand reflected memories.

Everyone who chooses to live in an old house is interested in recapturing some element of the charm and form of the past. This effort may extend to what is usually the most modern of rooms, the kitchen. In mixing the old and the new, however, every attempt must be made to keep from running amok in time. Too often a "colonial-style" kitchen with gate-leg table, large open fireplace fitted with crane and hanging pots, and a profusion of splint baskets is found in a late-Victorian home; similarly, such late 19th-century artifacts as the lazy Susan, steel milk can, and golden oak pillar table crop up in an 18th-century saltbox. Although few people who live comfortably with the past would expect (or could afford) to decorate with total historic fidelity, the contents of a room should reflect something of a house's true structural character and age. It is through the study of the past as revealed in its documents and artifacts that one can discover what is appropriate and not merely nostalgic.

The means used in cooking food has primarily determined the layout of the kitchen. From the early 17th century until the 1840s, wood was the fuel commonly employed in the fireplace. Coal was recognized by the mid-1800s as a much superior fuel for cook-

*Cooking methods common in the colonial period and early 19th century were still being followed in this isolated Alabama farmhouse when it was photographed in the 1930s. The shelf was added to the chimney long after the fireplace was built.*

stoves and ranges that were either inserted in the fireplace or installed elsewhere in the kitchen. From the 1880s to the 1930s, both gas and coal were employed for cooking in many homes, and sometimes the range was designed to burn both. Stoves continued to grow larger and larger and more sophisticated in operation with the use of more convenient and efficient fuel. The last revolution in cooking occurred in the 1930s when electricity first became widely available and economical in price.

The colonial period of American history is often seen as one static succession of years without significant technological change. On the contrary, the science of heating and cooking advanced continually, more rapidly in towns and cities than in the country, but markedly throughout the colonies. During most of the 17th century, a home was without a formal kitchen, the "hall," one of the two basic rooms of the average English colonial dwelling, serving as both kitchen and dining room. The fireplace in this room was the largest in the house, as wide as 8 to 12 feet in some cases, and certainly commodious enough for a wide variety of cooking utensils. The brick or stone hearth was the primary work area for the cook. The fireplace, also of brick or stone or a combination thereof, was properly vented with a chimney flue. The rear wall of the firebox was usually whitewashed. Iron firebacks were not commonly placed in a fireplace used for cooking; they found a more proper place in the parlor, a room, unlike the kitchen, unheated during a good portion of the day. A bake oven may have been built inside the kitchen fireplace or, more commonly, placed outside the house, attached to the chimney. Beehive

*One would hardly know that this was a kitchen. To emphasize the convenience of a gas stove in 1892, the artist chose to render a setting more like a parlor. The purveyors of electric appliances in the 1920s and '30s took similar liberty with the domestic scene in hopes of convincing the weary housewife that life in the kitchen could be beautiful.*

Below: *The raised panel fireplace wall of the kitchen in the William Brattle, Jr., House in Pittsfield, Mass., includes a bake oven behind a small paneled door to the left of the fireplace opening. The hearth extends the full width of the fireplace and projects 2½ feet into the room. The high-style Georgian colonial home was built in 1762.*

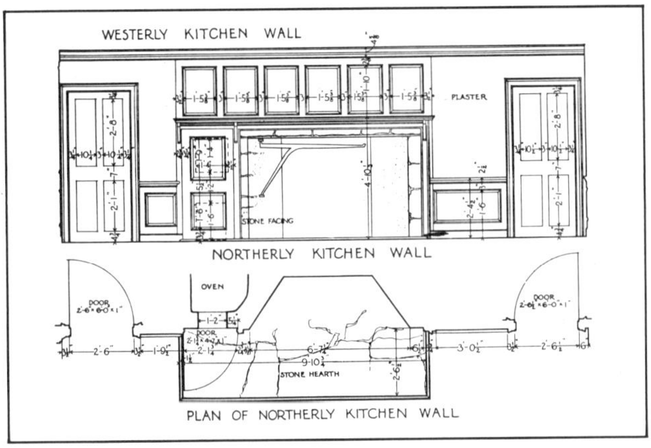

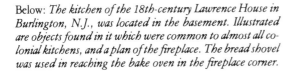

Below: *The kitchen of the 18th-century Lawrence House in Burlington, N.J., was located in the basement. Illustrated are objects found in it which were common to almost all colonial kitchens, and a plan of the fireplace. The bread shovel was used in reaching the bake oven in the fireplace corner.*

Above: *The original kitchen in the Nathaniel Macy House, Nantucket, Mass., built prior to 1745, was part of the "hall." The fireplace is approximately 10 feet wide and 3½ feet deep, adequate not only for cooking but even for warming oneself while seated on the bench to the side.*

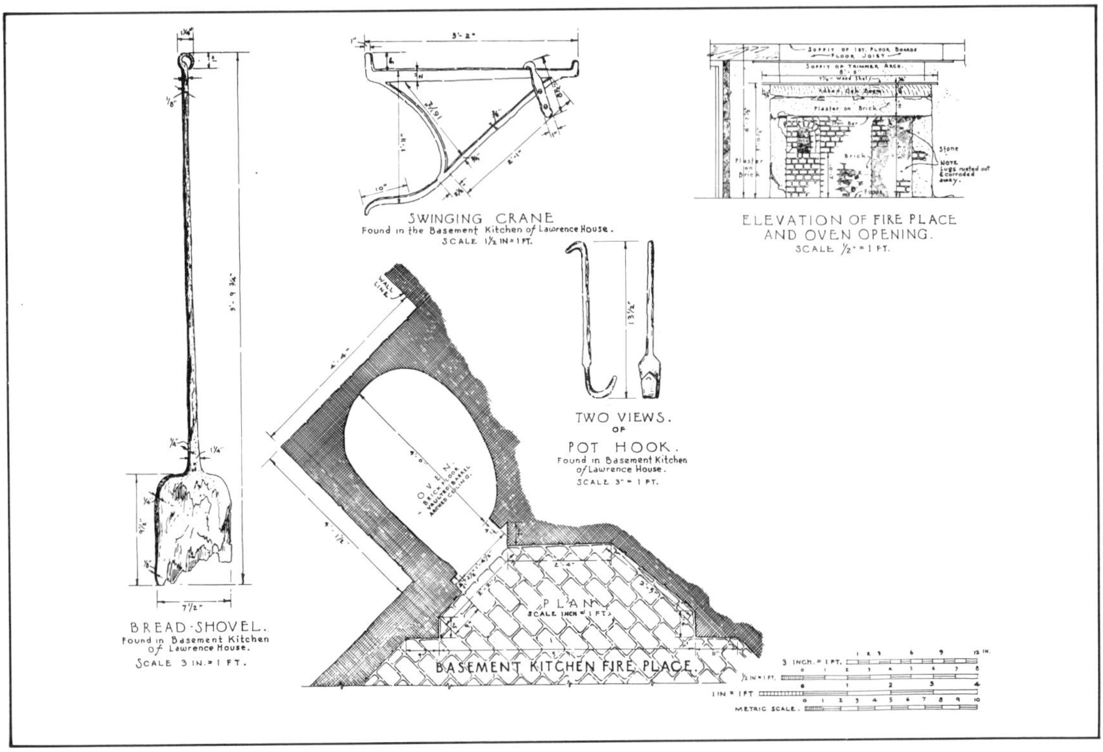

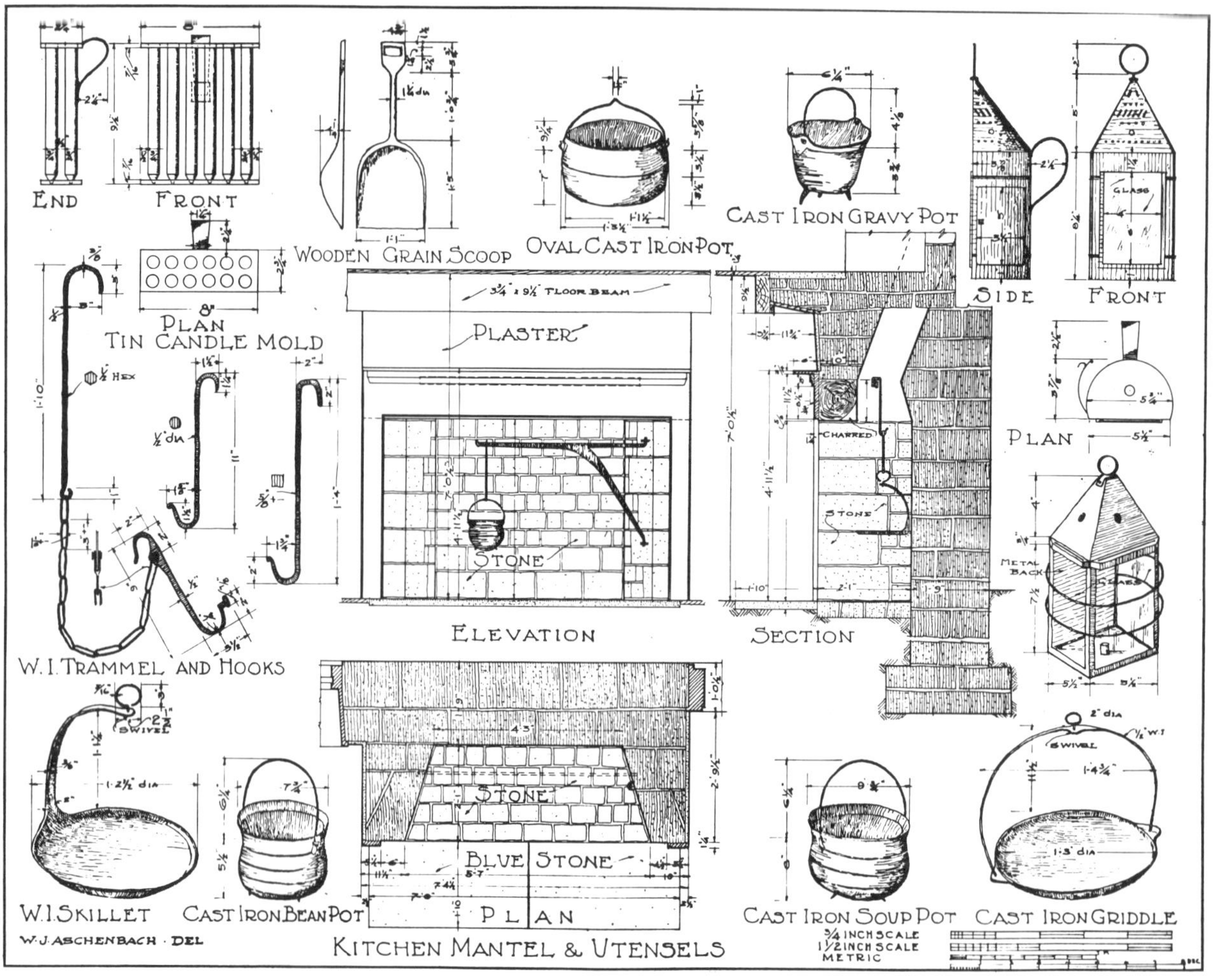

END
FRONT
TIN CANDLE MOLD
PLAN
WOODEN GRAIN SCOOP
OVAL CAST IRON POT
CAST IRON GRAVY POT
SIDE
FRONT
PLAN
GLASS
METAL BACK
3/4" x 9 1/2" FLOOR BEAM
PLASTER
STONE
ELEVATION
CHARRED
STONE
SECTION
W. I. TRAMMEL AND HOOKS
1/2" HEX
SWIVEL
STONE
BLUE STONE
PLAN
W. I. SKILLET
CAST IRON BEAN POT
CAST IRON SOUP POT
CAST IRON GRIDDLE
W. J. ASCHENBACH · DEL
KITCHEN MANTEL & UTENSELS
3/4 INCH SCALE
1 1/2 INCH SCALE
METRIC

ovens were common in early Virginia homes and were also known in the Spanish Southwest, although in the latter area they often stood alone, as illustrated on p. 44.

The earliest fireplaces were fitted with a fixed chimney bar or lug pole above the opening. From the pole, pothooks or trammels could be hung for suspending vessels. When iron cranes that could be pivoted out of the firebox opening began to be used in the late 17th century, the hanging of pots and kettles was made somewhat easier. Sometimes two cranes were used, one being attached to each side of the fireplace. Other indispensable pieces of hardware were andirons and spitdogs, the latter fitted with a series of hooks for attaching roasting spits. Rather sophisticated equipment was employed in some households for mechanically turning the spit. One such device was a clock jack with driving wheels and chain; another was a smoke jack that depended on smoke convection to activate a revolving paddle wheel. Yet another useful appliance was the tin or copper Dutch oven, a cylindrical half-box open to the fire and with a small door on the side facing the cook. The oven was fitted with a spit and used for roasting.

While any fireplace used for cooking was likely to have been fitted with a lug pole or a crane, few contained all of the ingenious devices which so fascinate us today. Virtually none was crowded with tools, implements, and utensils in the manner of many modern

Opposite page, top: *A clock jack used to turn a roasting spit is still in place in the 18th-century Major John Bradford House in Kingston, Mass. The bake oven rests alongside the fireplace.* Opposite page, bottom: *The utensils used in the kitchen of the 1706 Peter Van Duyne House in Wayne Township, N.J., were of wrought iron, wood, and cast iron. The pots and other devices could be suspended from a swinging crane by use of trammel hooks.* Below: *The great supporting beam for a fireplace was a convenient place from which to hang utensils. It was not a common resting place, most historians agree, for the trusty musket or a powder horn. For practical reasons, these objects were usually kept closer to the door.*

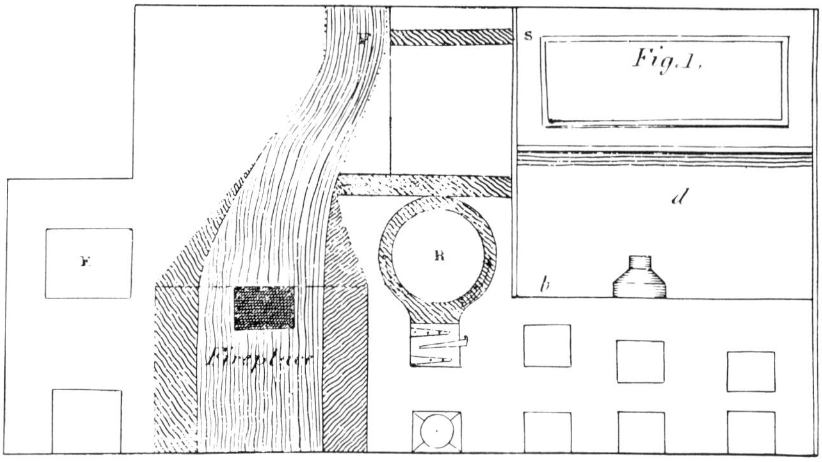


*Count Rumford, born Benjamin Thompson in Woburn, Mass., in 1753, was responsible for many improvements in cooking technology. Asher Benjamin included Rumford's design for a kitchen fireplace, oven (e), roaster (R), and boilers (d) in* The American Builder's Companion, *the first edition of which appeared in 1806. Rumford's designs were principally effective in improving heat retention.*

reconstructions. Trivets, gridirons, forks, ladles, spoons, and shovels were necessities, but were few in number and usually made of iron rather than more expensive brass or copper. Mantels were rare in the early years, and only in the 18th century did they appear in what might have been a new lean-to kitchen appended to an older building or in a separate kitchen outbuilding.

In North America wood remained the primary fuel for cooking—in both fireplaces and stoves—until the late 19th century; only in the cities or arid areas such as the Southwest or the Plains states was there a shortage. A plentiful supply, however, did not lessen the hard work of keeping a fire going day and night and the necessity of enough coals remaining in the early morning to build upon. There were constant attempts during the 17th and 18th centuries to improve upon the efficiency of the fireplace—drawing in the sides of the firebox at an angle to increase the draw of the fire, for example. A bake or warming oven was sometimes installed alongside the fireplace, being connected to the chimney flue or supplied with its own outlet. Despite these improvements, the fireplace remained an inefficient container for a fire; the iron heating stove, first introduced in the mid-18th century, was a more costly but logical next step in cooking technology.

Stoves were used for heating rooms before being adapted for cooking purposes. The equipment needed to prepare food more efficiently was not given much thought by those who paid servants to perform domestic services. Such labor was relatively inexpensive, and in some areas of the country was performed by black house servants. Yet even in those homes where the housewife was the cook, there was often a delay in making the switch from fireplace to a freestanding, enclosed stove. Although President Millard Fillmore introduced the first stoves to the Executive Mansion during his term of office in the early 1850s, it took several years before the White House cooks would make use of them.

Many cast-iron stoves were equipped to burn wood or coal, the latter fuel becoming increasingly popular during the 19th century because of its convenient size and efficiency. "Two good hodfuls" were considered all that

*The White House kitchen stoves introduced in the 1850s were replaced in the 1880s with a bank of coal-burning appliances. In 1901, the year this picture was taken, electricity was in use for lighting.*

was necessary for an ordinary day's supply in 1888. Starting and maintaining a fire each day, however, was still considerable work. Housewives were regularly advised in farm and home magazines on how to effectively regulate the drafts of a wood or coal stove. Nothing was considered more important to the kitchen than a constant supply of hot water and a fire was kept going to supply this need. If the stove was not built with an attached boiler, the common household kettle served the same purpose. Christine Herrick, the author of *Housekeeping Made Easy* (1888), stressed the importance of such a ready reserve with a story about an old lady who, "when dying and almost speechless, beckoned her daughter to bend over her to receive her final message, and murmured with her last breath, 'Always—keep—the—kettle—full—of—hot—water.'" The message, Miss Herrick underlined, "is not subject for ridicule to housewives."

Cast-iron cooking stoves became more

*A coal hod, either open (at left) or with a funnel (at right), was usually stationed close to the stove. It had to be filled at least several times a day from a bin located in the basement or, more conveniently, in a storage area next to the kitchen.*

Above: *A reservoir for hot water was provided on most stoves, wood or coal, made after the mid-19th century. This 1888 model, made by Thomas, Roberts & Stevenson, Philadelphia, came with a cast white enameled or copper reservoir; the reservoir is the extension to the right of the oven.* Right: *The "Majestic" was a first-class coal-burning range that, the manufacturer claimed, would "pay for itself in the saving of fuel in a short time."* A range *included an oven and burners, whereas a* stove *was often without provision for baking.* Below: *The kitchen in the "Old Manse," Concord, Mass., where Nathaniel Hawthorne once lived, dates from 1769. The firebox was bricked in during the 19th century with only a hole left for the stove pipe. The boiler to the right of the range was probably installed at the same time.*

and more elaborate over the years with the addition of special linings, hot water reservoirs, draft controls, and grates adaptable for wood or coal. A new stove was, understandably, a family's prize possession. Placement of the ever-larger contraptions varied from house to house. In older homes, the stove was often placed just inside the fireplace opening; in new homes, fireplaces were sometimes eliminated and the stove was merely vented through the roof with a long extension of stove pipe and a special collar and pipe. A "range breast," or special chimney recess for a kitchen without a fireplace, was recommended in the 1860s by some writers. It was important in the days before gas or electric refrigeration to isolate as much of the heat of a stove as possible, especially during the warm months. During this time of the year, it was often the practice to disassemble the stove and reinstall it in a separate building, commonly called a summer kitchen.

By the 1880s stoves had been universally adopted and kerosene and gas were other

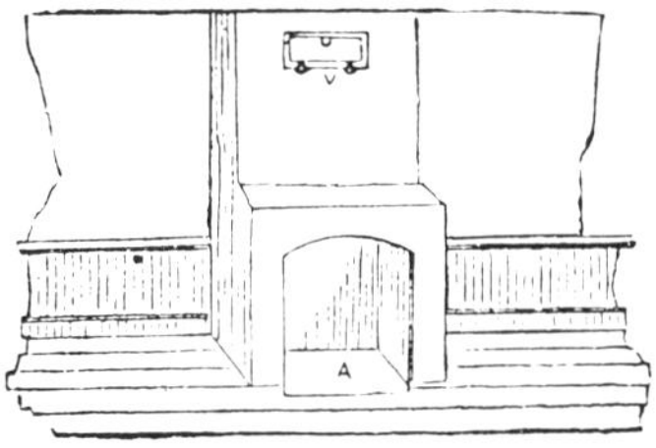


Above: *Architect Daniel T. Atwood provided this design for a range breast in his* Country and Suburban Homes *(1871). He advised that it be built "instead of the common stove chimney . . . in order that the gases and vapor made while . . . cooking . . . be taken immediately from the room."* Below: *Coal ranges continued to be used in many homes, at least for baking, after the introduction of gas. The photograph dates from the early 1900s, a time when cooking with gas was still a novelty.*

*As late as World War II, many farm families still depended on a wood or coal-burning appliance. This 1940 photograph from the Farm Security Administration archives shows a North Dakota housewife at work on a well-kept Janney, Semple & Hill Co. "Service Malleable."*

possible alternative fuels for use. Gas was the most efficient fuel yet introduced and was a practical alternative in urban areas. Wood or coal continued to be used widely in rural areas until the 1920s because of their portability and low cost. There were, however, prosperous country households equipped with their own gas installations, but these generally provided only fuel for lighting and heating hot water.

Beginning in the mid-1800s, almost all building contractors included a cookstove in their specifications. Those in A.J. Bicknell's *Village Builder* (1872) are typical: "Put in the kitchen a range to cost not less than seventy-five dollars, to be chosen by the owner." Floor plans drawn up before the Civil War rarely include any indication of the placement of a stove, water heater, or sink; only the location of the fireplace is noted. Gradually, more and more of the elements of a modern kitchen were filled in. By the early 1900s the kitchen was becoming rather crowded with permanent appliances and fixtures. Cupboards were now being built into place with work counters below them; sinks were supplied with side drainboards of enameled iron. The concept of a kitchen as a "laboratory" and as an adjunct of modern "domestic science" was taking hold. At a time when servants were becoming more difficult to find and expensive to keep, housewives avidly studied the recommendations of professionals for saving steps in the preparation of meals. The model kitchen was one in which there was to be a "work triangle," the points of which were the refrigerator, sink, and stove. If the stove was the newly-invented electric range, all the better since the appliance was the cleanest known to date. In addition, a *House and Garden* writer argued in 1915, "This item . . . is cheaper in labor than gas or coal."

*"An Electric Kitchen," as illustrated in* The House and Home, A Practical Book *(1896). A collection of appliances took the place of a range; each gadget is plugged in separately. A roasting oven stands on the floor next to this odd electric banquette.*

In order to encourage the use of electric ranges in the 1920s and '30s, manufacturers adopted the streamlined modular designs of such stylists as Norman Bel Geddes. There was a conscious attempt to fit the appliance into the modern, efficient order of things. This meant a smaller, more compact unit that could be easily accommodated in the flow of cupboards and work spaces. The lighter, white enameled steel body of the range was as bright and hygienic as any meticulous housewife could desire. It was not long before the gas range was also redesigned along similar lines.

In succeeding years there was not to be any radical change in cooking technology until the introduction of the microwave oven. The use of many time-saving electric appliances —refrigerators, dishwashers, mixers, toasters, blenders—did, of course, alter the methods of food preparation, as did the advance in frozen food processing and the availability of prepared "fast foods." But, despite the sometimes startling changes in styling over the years, the basic kitchen design first promoted in the early 1900s and based on the three basic related work areas—the "work triangle"—has been only slightly altered by these improvements in preparation and processing.

*How could one fail to show off a range so clean and efficient as this model from Westinghouse, c. 1940? It was the centerpiece of a truly modern kitchen.*

# 2.
# A Place for Everything and Everything in Its Place

Homes became more complex and specialized in the division of living space and its use from the colonial period until the early 20th century. As families acquired more wealth, larger and larger dwellings were built and their layout allowed for an increasing number of social and practical needs. Space for the storage of cooking and dining supplies and accessories was among the improvements most often sought during this period. In the 17th century a corner cupboard in the "hall," a room which served as both the principal living area and as the kitchen, may have held a family's eating utensils and serving dishes; wooden barrels and boxes were often used for basic foodstuffs. Two hundred years later, a well-equipped kitchen contained at least open shelves and a multipurpose cabinet; adjoining the room was often a pantry where china and glass could be kept along with various staples. Only after World War I did such an amenity as a pantry begin to disappear from model house plans. By this time, new time-saving appliances were beginning to change the housewife's routine. Modern kitchen design, incorporating such improvements, allowed for space to be used more efficiently, and there was no longer a need for other storage areas.

The first several generations of settlers in North America had little money to spend on generous living space and the items needed to make housework easier. There was little space in most early homes for storing foodstuffs or provision for preserving the most perishable for very long. The colonists' need for storage space and for places to preserve staples, however, was much greater than that of the late Victorians who enjoyed the luxury of the icebox and pantry. Foodstuffs were often purchased or produced in bulk and had to be kept for some time under primitive conditions.

A completely separate room for cooking was one of the first to be added to the early 17th-century house and was included in a majority of new homes built from the 1720s in urban and rural areas. Since there was no precedent to follow in furnishing such a specialized space, it is not surprising to discover that the first kitchen was virtually formless compared with that known later. In both town and farm houses, shelves were hung here and there and were usually plain pine boards nailed up in a corner; the fireplace was the only "appliance" in sight.

The country kitchen was usually placed on the main floor or comprised a separate nearby building. Cellar space was often more limited than in the town house since perish-

*Stratford Hall, the historic Lee family estate in Westmoreland County, Va., dates from 1725-30 and has a separate two-story kitchen building. Today it is more lavishly and neatly furnished than it would have been in the 18th century. Since the property is a house museum, it is important to display as many of the common utensils and furnishings as possible, although in the 18th century cooking would have been impossible with so many objects in the fireplace.*

ables could be kept in outside dugouts. The smokehouse was a place for both curing and storing meat; the dairy or springhouse provided a cool spot for milk products.

The typical town house kitchen was located in the basement or "half-basement" that rose partially above ground level. This was the coolest area of the house, which, if not supplied with proper ventilation and light, could be a rather dank and cheerless area. Potatoes, carrots, cabbages, and onions might be stored in an adjoining room or "closet." Many city dwellers cultivated small vegetable gardens, and some kept a cow and chickens as well as pigs for slaughter. In 18th-century Williamsburg, for example, one was as likely to meet a pig rooting along the street as a periwigged gentleman out for a stroll. Despite such familiarity with the raw ingredients of daily consumption, however, the urban housewife or housekeeper stored much less than her country counterpart. By the mid-18th century, the city dweller could find a wide variety of goods in the public markets.

It was the newly-affluent merchant class of the cities and the wealthy landowners of the rural coastal areas of the North and South who were to bring about striking changes in the form of the house and use of its space from the 1720s to the early 19th century. Both groups shared an admiration for the ordered Georgian style of life of the English upper class, and could afford to emulate its example. As Americans acquired finer and more specialized possessions, and improved their diet with a greater selection and quality of foods, the layout of the houses in which they lived also evolved. Bare-bones kitchens were supplied with freestanding cupboards and special storage containers for such staples

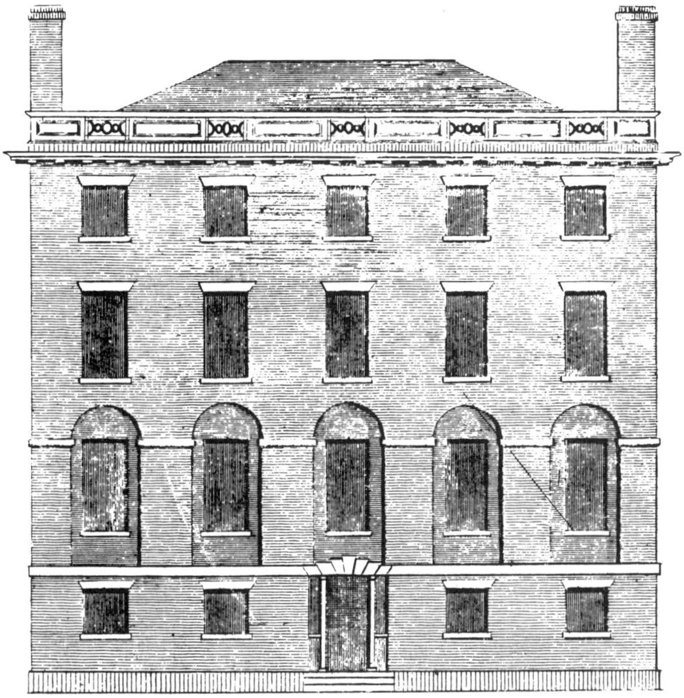

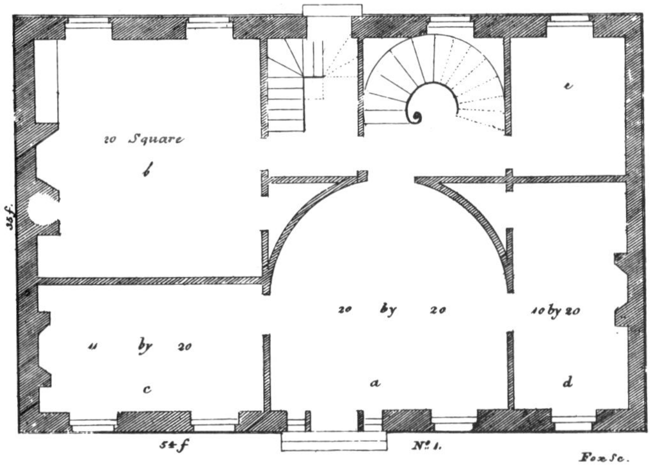


as spices, sugar, and tea. New homes were built with separate formal dining rooms and a series of service areas linking up with the kitchen; many old houses were remodeled in a similar manner.

The dining room is the most visible symbol of the change in life style. It was the place in which to exhibit one's degree of social status as measured in china, silver, and glass. These objects could be displayed in a built-in cupboard, a sideboard, or china cabinet. Some of the pieces would be used at the table, although probably only when company was present. More common tablewares were stored in an adjoining pantry or in the kitchen.

The pantry, introduced in the late 1700s, grew in size and importance throughout the 19th century. Much that is stored in a kitchen today—flour, sugar, cooking oil, and other staples—was carefully housed there. Shelves were often arranged from floor to ceiling, and some of them were fitted out with doors that could be locked against thievery. The present-day owner of a large 18th-century Southern plantation house remembers going with her mother and the housekeeper to a "locked pantry" early each morning to remove the provisions needed by the cook for

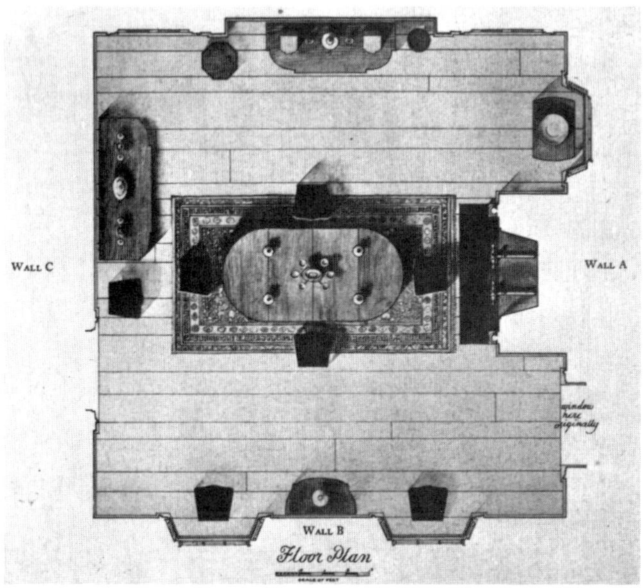


Top: *Asher Benjamin's design for a town house, included in* The American Builder's Companion *(1806), placed the kitchen on the half-basement level where one also entered the building.* Center: *As seen in the floor plan, the kitchen (b) is a 20-foot square room supplied only with fireplace and bake oven. Two windows, each of six panes, provided natural light.* Bottom: *The layout of the dining room at Oak Hill, an Essex County, Mass., country house built in 1801, was basically simple and similar to that found in other parts of the country during the first half of the 19th century. The large room was not crowded with furniture, but contained only a table, chairs, a sideboard, buffet, and two small side tables.*

Left: *The icebox changed little during the 19th century. This model, of ash, was insulated with charcoal sheathing and lined with metal. It was offered in the 1897 Sears, Roebuck catalogue.* Below: *The authors of* Village and Farm Cottages *(1856)—Henry W. Cleaveland, William Backus, and Samuel D. Backus—considered the kitchen the "heart of a farmhouse. Around this, all other things must range themselves." As seen in the floor plan, the kitchen with fireplace (k) was large enough to serve as a dining room; adjoining it are a small pantry (p) equipped with pump, sink, and shelves, and a washroom (w.r.), containing an oven and boiler.*

the day. Hanging from the ceiling on hooks were hams, smoked tongues, and dried beef wrapped in whitewashed cloths.

The pantry was also the place where the first icebox or refrigerator might have been placed. As Eliza Leslie, the author of *The House Book,* counseled in 1844, it should stand away from "any place where there is fire," meaning cooking heat. For the same reason, a pantry was also a suitable place for a safe, another word for a locked cupboard and defined by Miss Leslie as "standing on feet; the doors and sides being made of wire net or of perforated tin." It contained shelves and was used "for keeping cold meat, pies, and other articles left from the table."

If a home was not supplied with a pantry in the 19th century, and many were not, there was likely to be an area designated as a "scullery," storeroom, or laundry. In such a modest dwelling, there was no need for a way-station for a maid or a butler between kitchen and dining room. The extra room off the kitchen was a place where things could be kept out of sight, where pots and pans could be scrubbed, and the laundry done. Since closets were rarely provided in the kitchen proper, save one for brooms and brushes, a back room was a convenient storage area for

FIRST STORY PLAN.

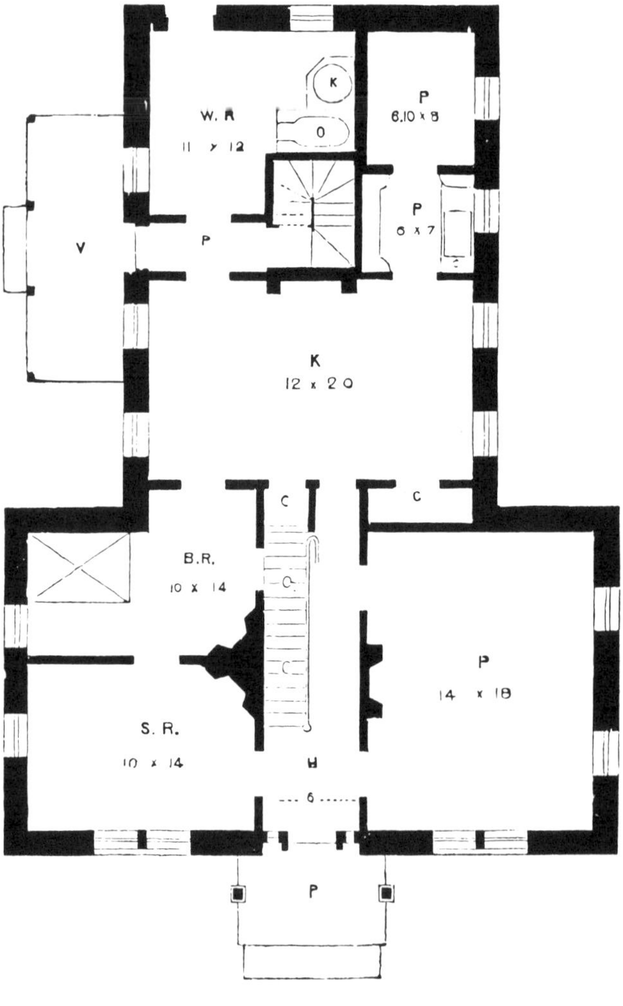

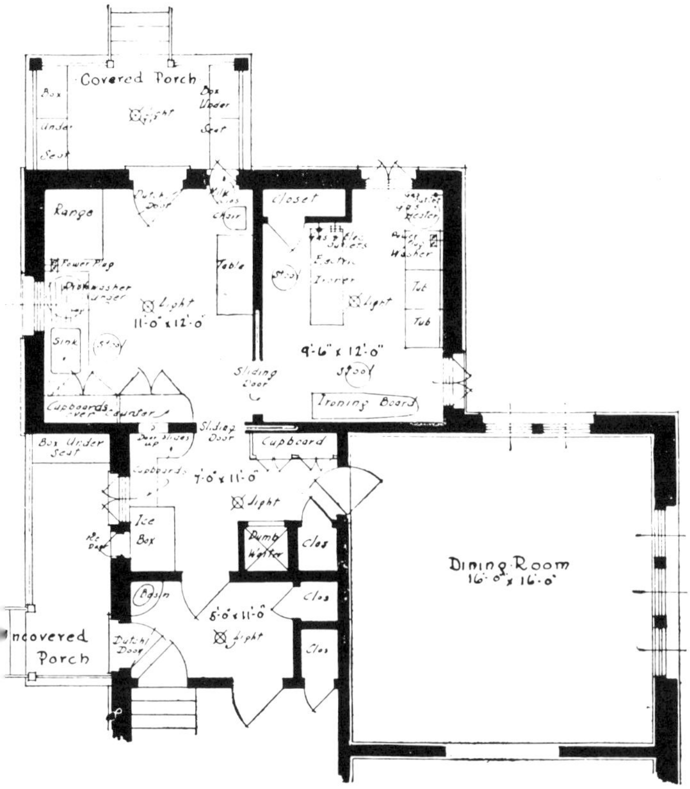


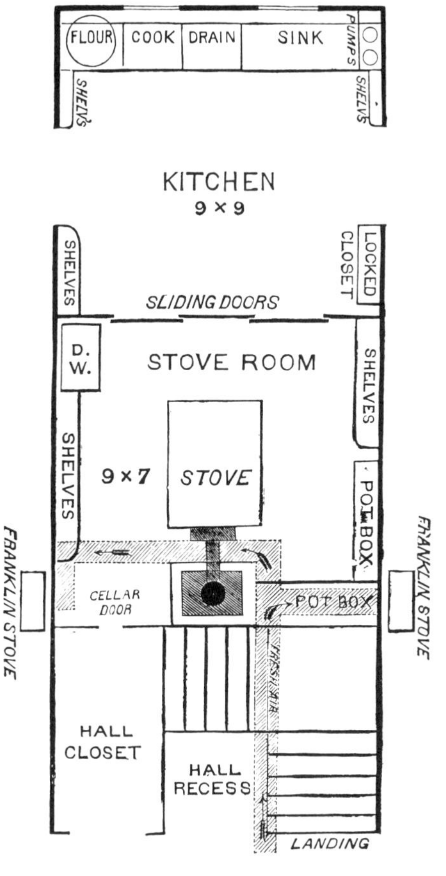


preserves and basic foodstuffs and, later, tinned goods. Here the daily "help," and not a live-in servant, could also keep supplies for housecleaning at the ready. The back room was, as well, a suitable place for an icebox; in homes of limited space, however, the icebox was usually placed on a porch.

During the 20th century both the pantry and the back room disappeared in new homes. This was as much a result of the loss of "help," an economic problem, as it was the improvement in the methods of food preparation and preservation. As packaged foods became more and more common, there was less need to store large quantities of staples. Improved refrigeration techniques made it easier to plan meals on more than a day-to-day basis and offered a greater variety of readily available items. All of this was a godsend to the average housewife in the early 1900s who, while probably not a suffragette, shared with other women a longing to be free of many tiring kitchen duties. Her wants and desires had been carefully studied by experts in "domestic science" in teacher's colleges and cooking schools across the country since the late 19th century. Suggestions on how to improve the layout of the kitchen came as rapidly during the early 1900s as the introduction of more efficient appliances.

Above: *In a 1921 article entitled "A Well-Planned Kitchen Helps to Solve the Servant Problem," a* Country Life *writer strongly urged that the pantry be included in the modern house plan. The kitchen proper (the room at top left) was to include a dishwasher, sink, range, and built-in cupboards; it was felt that a cool pantry (to the left of the dining room) was necessary for the icebox and foodstuffs.* Below: *The Beecher sisters, Catherine E. and Harriet Beecher Stowe, had many suggestions to make for improving kitchen design in* The American Woman's Home *(1869). Cooking and preparing food were functions that were separated in their model floor plan. Ample space was provided for storage in each area.*

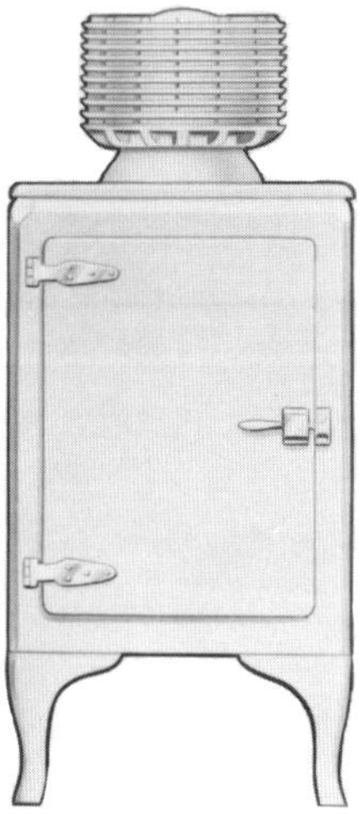

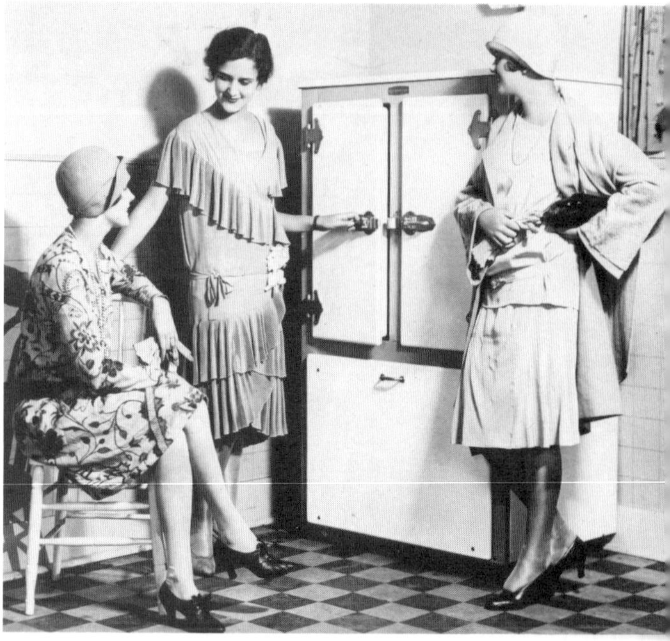

Above: *General Electric's "monitor-top" refrigerator was introduced in the late 1920s and became a classic symbol of modern American appliance design. The first universally popular electric refrigerator, it was sturdy and compact and was easy to clean under its Chippendale legs.* Right: *An electric refrigerator, in this case a Frigidaire, could be placed almost anywhere in the kitchen. In contrast, the icebox had to be kept far away from any source of heat.*

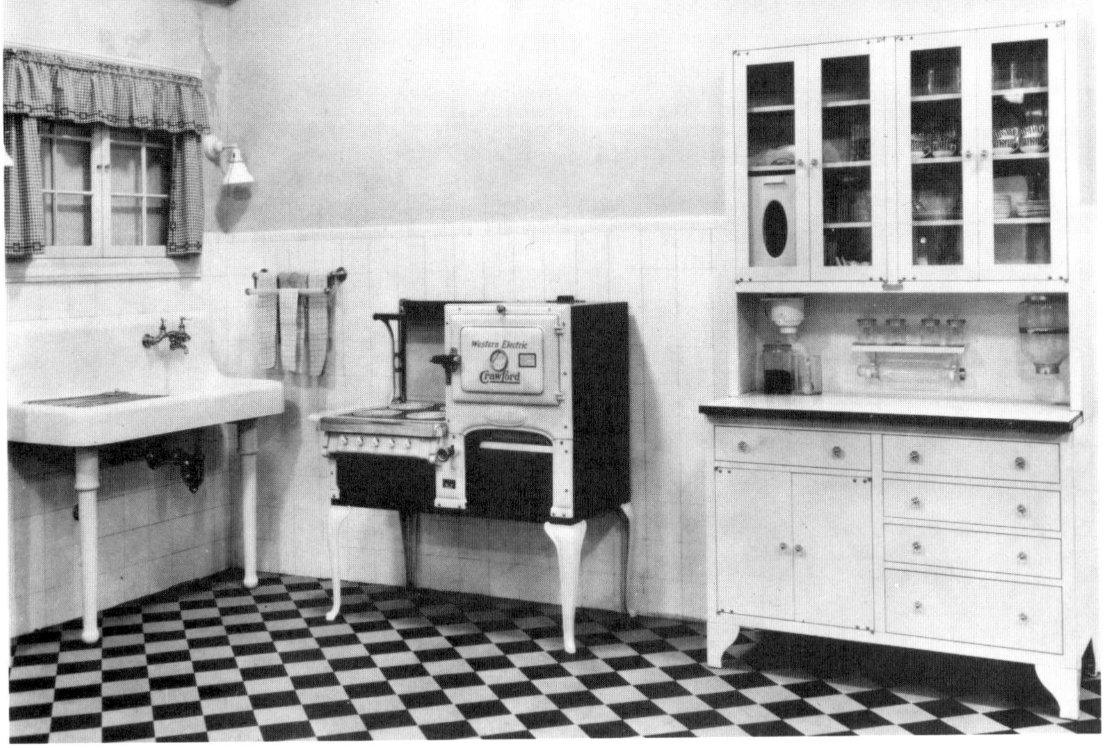


Opposite page, below: *In 1976 two types of freestanding cupboards or cabinets were still in use in the kitchen of the 1867 Galbraith House, Idaho City, Idaho. The older of the two stands next to a broom closet built below the chimney flue. It does not appear that the room was ever supplied with a fireplace.* Above: *The cabinet chosen by many housewives in the early 1900s was an up-to-date metal version of the wood cupboard. Crockery was stored on the upper shelves, and utensils and table linen in the lower drawers. Dispensers for flour (left) and sugar (right) were often built in.*

The "modern" housewife—wealthy or average in income—wished to have all that she needed for preparing meals close at hand. This need was clearly understood by such a pioneer of contemporary furniture and house design as Gustav Stickley in 1909: "Ample cupboard space for all china should be provided near the sink to do away with unnecessary handling, and the same cupboard, which should be an actual structural feature of the kitchen, should contain drawers for table linen, cutlery, and small utensils. . . ." A freestanding cupboard, earlier termed a dresser, had been used in many kitchens for years, but what Stickley had in mind was something closer to the multipurpose cabinet with various storage areas popularized by such mail-order concerns as Sears and Montgomery Ward. "So convenient is a cabinet of this kind," enthused home economist Clara Laughlin in *The Complete Home* (1912), "and so economical of steps, that it might be called 'the complete housewife.'" The next logical step, as Stickley suggested, was to "build-in" such conveniences. Kitchen plans had grown more detailed throughout the 19th century, but rarely included more than a sink, stove, and boiler; plans prepared by post-World War I builders often called for a sink, stove, refrigerator, and counter and cabinet units.

Because cooking and preservation technology changed so radically during the early 20th century, kitchens found in houses built before this time are often odd-looking creations. They may be composed of parts adopted at various times—a modern electric stove and refrigerator, freestanding wood or

enameled steel cabinets, an open rather than enclosed sink. Often the situation is so chaotic that only a new modular design will suffice. In remodeling such a room most home owners wisely refrain from attempting a period "restoration" since to be true to almost any period of the past would require a return to an inefficient arrangement ill-suited to today's needs.

Primary attention must be given in redoing a kitchen to the disposition of the most commonly used elements—appliances, utensils, and basic foodstuffs—so that they may be employed with relative ease. It may be possible to make use of functional objects from the past. Among the most useful are those designed for storage—hanging wall and freestanding cupboards, multipurpose cabinets, and safes. Appropriately selected antique furnishings can be integrated in almost any modern arrangement without sacrificing efficiency.

Opposite page: *A multipurpose kitchen cabinet from Sears was advertised in 1927 as "The Happiest Surprise of Her Life!" The enameled wood behemoth included containers for coffee, tea, spices, flour, and sugar, a breadboard and drawer, a block for chopping, a meal bin, hooks for hanging billls, and various trays and holders.* Right: *Built-in cupboards above and below counters took the place of free-standing cabinets in the totally remodeled 20th-century kitchen. Even in a new home, however, it was difficult to know what to do with electric cords; there were never enough convenient outlets.* Below: *"Asleep at the Switch" was the title of a film short produced by Radio Pictures in 1930. Mechanization had taken over and there was nothing left for the housewife to do but turn the knobs in her all-electric kitchen.*

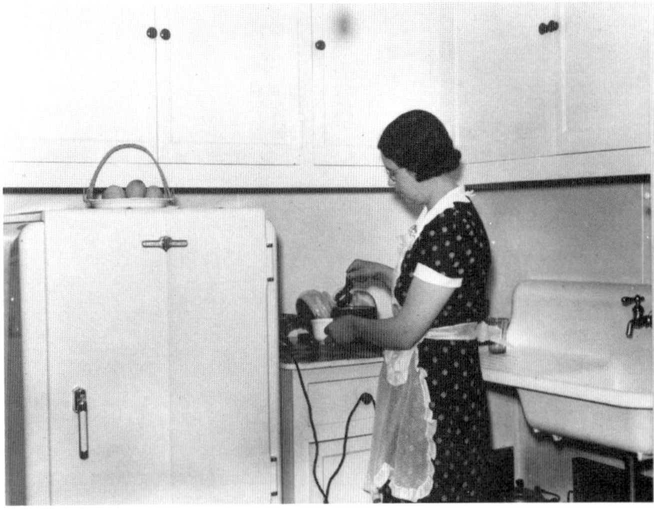

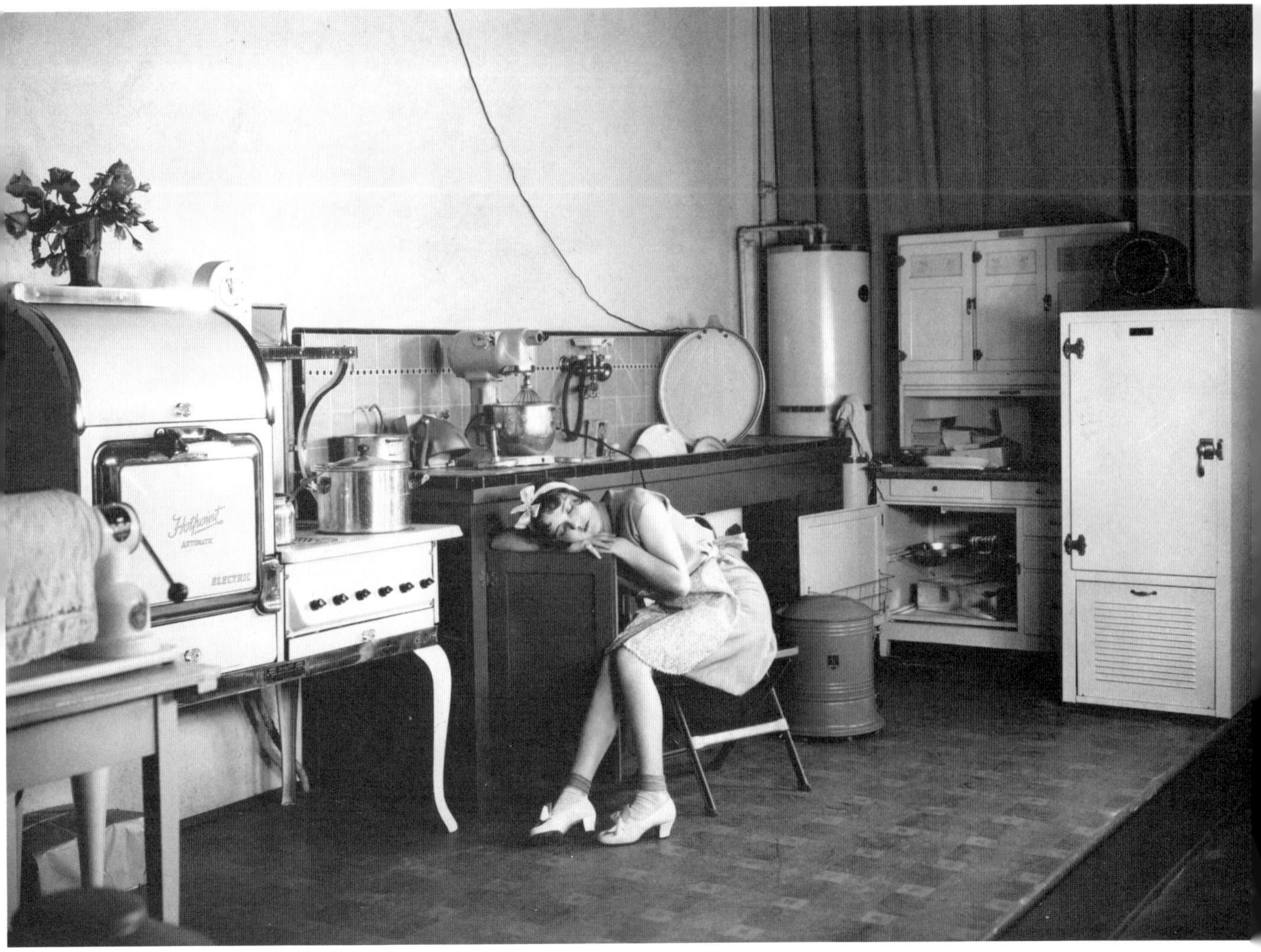

# 3.
# A Portfolio of Period Kitchens and Dining Rooms

Tracing the development of the kitchen and dining room in America over a 350-year period brings to light a complex interplay of geographic, technological, economic, social, and aesthetic factors. History is never easy to sort out, and a clear-cut presentation of a particular period, as in the manner of a museum "model" room, is often misleading. The dining room has not changed drastically over time, but the kitchen has undergone considerable revision over the past 200 years. The rooms illustrated in the following pages, some modern, others less touched by time, and all from presently lived-in private homes throughout the United States, do not fit into neat categories of time and place. There is about each of them, however, a considered reflection of some past practices and taste in use of materials and forms and a realistic concern for present-day utility. These rooms have been grouped together regionally—the Northeast, Southwest, Old South, Mid-South, and Far West—in order to point out certain common building practices, and, to some extent, the rooms within a region are related to each other stylistically. Consciously eliminated from this selection are rooms which are more a reflection of a desire for charm than authenticity. The pages of contemporary decorating magazines are filled with pictures of the familiar cosy kitchens and dining rooms in which baskets, flowers, pillows, and matched sets of cookware are used in place of more substantial and fitting objects. The following pages, to the contrary, should prove that it is possible for the old and new to coexist without being self-consciously contrived.

---

Left and opposite page: *A modest 1720-30 southeast Massachusetts "half-house" with a gable-end chimney was moved and reerected in the 1970s. Now there are two first-floor rooms rather than one, but the kitchen and dining room remain combined. A long pine trestle table and an oriental rug define the dining area. The kitchen equipment is thoroughly modern, yet through the use of old pine these 20th-century appurtenances blend in harmoniously with the antique. The Victorian slate sink comes from another old house.*

# *The Northeast*

Homes in the area reaching from northern New England through the Middle Atlantic states are among the oldest in the country. Although the Southwest was explored at an earlier time, few vestiges of the established Spanish Colonial culture of this period remain to be studied. In contrast, almost any given town in the coastal areas of Massachusetts, New York State, or New Jersey is likely to contain houses which date at least from the 18th century; there may be dozens which were built, in large part, from the late 1800s through the first decades of the 19th century. Few are pure in period style since they have changed ownership many times, with each successive owner having made what he considered to be decorative and/or structural improvements. A separate kitchen, for example, was often added to a 17th-century house in the following century; a dining room may have been carved out of previously existing space in the early 19th century, or, as in the case of the room illustrated on p. 38, added as recently as the 1930s. Only two of the homes from the Northeast shown in these pages—the 1803 Newport, R.I., house on p. 35 and the 1845-47 New York City town house on p. 42—were built originally with a separate dining room. In addressing problems of restoration, compromise in style is as necessary as economy in almost all instances. There are no easy answers to structural and design problems which have been tackled by many generations of home owners.

*In the neighborhood of the Massachusetts home previously illustrated is one begun in the late 17th century and substantially enlarged in the 1720s in the early Georgian style. The kitchen was placed in one rear corner of the house, connecting with a front dining room-sitting room. Now it is completely equipped with up-to-date appliances and storage space. The basic structural lines of the room, with exposed framing, have been followed in accommodating the cabinets, slate sink, and dishwasher. The materials used in the remodeling carefully match the old. Above the stove area is an antique built-in pine cupboard. It has been placed in a position originally occupied by a window that had to be removed when the house gained a rear addition. Not visible to the left are glass doors added to bring more light into the room; their scale is somewhat out of proportion with the other structural elements, but the lines are simple enough not to detract from the room's basic character and the gain in cheerful sunlight is appreciable.*

*The rear left-corner room of this 1803 Newport, R.I., town house has always served as the kitchen. The cupboards and appliances are modern, but the original paneled fireplace still serves a practical function. It was probably used for open-fire cooking until the mid-19th century, and then converted to accommodate a cook stove, which would also have served to heat the room. Today our need is for inexpensive heating that cannot be supplied by a modern insulated cook stove. Proving remarkably effective in this home is an Ashley Automatic Heater, made in Sheffield, Ala., around the turn of the century. A fireboard covers up the fireplace opening in the manner originally intended for a cookstove.*

*The 1760 Williamson-Sickles homestead in rural Monmouth County, N.J., was originally only a one-room-wide dwelling, the first floor containing a parlor and sitting room-kitchen, and the second floor two bedrooms. In the mid-1800s a new kitchen wing was added to the side, almost doubling the size of the house and making room for a dining room in the former kitchen. The massive stone corner fireplace wall with built-in cupboards is without mantel or any other adornment, an appearance that is well-documented in similar New Jersey houses built by the Dutch during the colonial period. The room is furnished in a manner that would have been common in the first half of the 19th century. The early Windsor chairs are thought to have come from the Imlay house in Allentown, N.J., and the table is termed a "hutch" table.*

*When discovered in the 1930s, this suburban Fairfield County, Conn., Cape had not changed drastically in at least 100 years. The original 1750s section, seen in the black and white photograph in the right foreground, may have been two-rooms wide and one-room deep, the hall first serving as the kitchen and dining room. Somewhat later, a lean-to portion was built, including a separate kitchen and back parlor. The dining room shown here was added along with a pantry and kitchen in the 1930s. Behind it, through the French doors, is an extension of the back parlor which serves as a garden room. Old beams were used in the ceiling and antique timber in framing the walls, and appropriate period lighting fixtures cast a pleasing amount of light. The oval drop-leaf table is of the kind often used for dining before the introduction of the extension table in the 1850s.*

*The appointments used on and around the dining table of this Bucks County, Pa., home reflect the special taste of the owner, a collector of American and English antiques. An eclectic approach to furnishing a period room is often difficult to sustain in a house with distinct period architectural character. This structure, a converted 1830s canal boathouse, was and remains, however, a study in stylistic minimalism. The only distinctive architectural element is the board and batten siding of the exterior. The fireplace is original to the period, and was used for cooking and heating when the building served as both a place where barges were built and workers lived. The floor was at first nothing more than earth, the random-width pine having been added in the 1920s conversion. At the same time, the floor was stippled by artist Alan Saalberg with the use of elephant-ear sponges.*

*The American Empire mahogany dining table used in the Bucks County home has ten leaves and folds up into a card table; it comes from an early 19th-century Hudson Valley estate. The set of American Queen Anne chairs dates from the mid-1700s. In the background is an oak Queen Anne Welsh dresser from England.*

*The small galley kitchen was carved out of one corner of the boathouse's new dining room. Because of its size and limited light, it is painted in a single bright color. Since the home is used mainly for weekends, a lavishly equipped space is not necessary. An open floor plan, merging kitchen and dining room, had been considered, but this gesture to convenience and modernism might have detracted from the dining room's pleasant air of formality.*

*Very careful thought has gone into the conversion of a first-floor butler's pantry to a working kitchen. The original kitchen of the 1845-47 Andrew Norwood house in New York City was located in the basement, just below the dining room. This arrangement was common in 18th and 19th-century town houses since land was at a premium and service wings could not extend in all directions. Food was brought to the dining level by dumbwaiter. Each floor of this restored house is now a separate apartment supplied with the necessities of modern life. When restoration began, there was little left of the original pantry except for its fine architectural detailing, but the owner has most successfully rebuilt it in the style of a galley kitchen and Victorian butler's hideaway. The mahogany cabinets and serpentine marble counter are new; so, too, is the Carrara marble floor. A chef's stove is tucked away in an alcove near the rear entryway. Not visible to the left of the stove is the refrigerator.*

Opposite page: *Cabinetwork of this quality will last as long as the house itself and increase in value with it. The limited amount of preparation, cooking, and clean-up space reflects the owner's own daily needs, which are minimal.*

# *The Southwest*

The adobe houses of the Southwest are seemingly timeless. To the unpracticed eye, it is difficult to know the age of a particular house or to determine when and where an addition such as a kitchen or dining room might have been made. Historians are quick, however, to point out the differences between various building periods as evidenced in the use of millwork, roofing materials, flooring, and window sash. Only the kitchen illustrated on this page is from a home that can be documented as being at least 225 to 250 years old; the other rooms are from houses built or completely rebuilt in the 1920s and '30s. The malleable, sculptural quality of adobe clay lends to these buildings a continuous form even when the expanded floor plan is that of an L or inverted U. It is known, however, that the first ranch houses were only one-room deep and probably no wider. Cooking, eating, sleeping—all took place in this one large space. Gradually, room was added to room in a long line of succession, and finally the corners were turned 90 degrees to form what is now considered a classic hacienda with a courtyard at its center. In such an arid climate, the outdoors was always within easy reach of the string of chambers; the courtyard or patio was itself considered an outdoor living and dining room. Baking was often done outside rather than in the kitchen.

*The kitchen may have been the first of the rooms to be added to the Ignacio de Roybal house in the Pojoaque Valley near Santa Fe, N.M. The room as it appears now bears no resemblance to the original space. Nevertheless, the materials used in it so handsomely—the weathered wood cabinets and butcher block, the unglazed Mexican tiles on the walls and the floor, the scattering of Indian clay pots—compose a period statement of undeniable character and charm, one perfectly in keeping with the basic traditional structure of the room.*

*The vast dining hall of this adobe ranch house north of Albuquerque in the Rio Grande Valley took its present form in the 1920s. Heiress Ruth Hanna McCormick Simms and her husband, Albert "discovered" New Mexico at that time, and had the good fortune to employ a young architect, John Gaw Meem, to transform the run-down structure into the handsome center of a large working ranch. The dining room stands on the foundations of the original horizontally-extended building. Meem, a master of the Pueblo/Spanish Revival style, invested the whole structure—with an addition extending from each side at a 90-degree angle—with the graceful artifacts of the 18th-century builders. The corner Pueblo fireplace, the high ceiling defined by cedar vigas or beams, and the tiled floor of the immense sparsely-furnished dining room combine to create an almost monastic atmosphere. In such a setting Spanish-Colonial armchairs and a refectory table are most appropriate furnishings.*

*A well-equipped kitchen designed in the 1920s has a certain attraction today. That found in the New Mexico ranch house illustrated here and on the previous page has hardly changed in more than fifty years. In the days before everything was enclosed within a streamlined unit, appliances boldly stated what they were for and how they worked. Nickel chrome and baked enamel were lavished on the most mundane objects and lent them an air of cleanliness and practicality. Early 20th-century kitchen appliances have proved remarkably durable because of the fine materials that went into their making.*

*Massive, multi-layered homes built between the world wars in what New Mexicans term the Pueblo/Spanish Revival style are to be found in Santa Fe's central and best residential district. They are as typical of the wealthy builders' preoccupation with grandeur and old-world bearing as the "Stockbroker Tudor" homes of Shaker Heights and the Mission-style homes of West Hollywood. Kitchens are immense and, as in the case of the Albuquerque ranch previously illustrated, were furnished with every conceivable type of appliance and storage facility. The kitchen of this house occupies one corner of a sprawling first floor set on several levels and divided into usable space by wide archways. Seen behind the kitchen is a laundry area, and beyond that the service entryway. Small floor tiles, glazed green tiles for the counters, a corner oven range with a conical hood in the form of a Pueblo fireplace, and a punched tin hanging light fixture are all minor but attractive and useful elements in the room's decor.*

# *The Old South*

The homes of the oldest part of the South, a region beginning in tidewater Maryland and reaching down the coast to Georgia, are about as varied in style as those found in other areas of early settlement. The abundant Georgian colonial and ante-bellum plantation houses, however, set this region apart from others in architectural character. These homes were often built in separate units of rooms connected by covered or open walkways, Washington's Mount Vernon being a conspicuous example. In such a warm climate, it was practical to house the kitchen separately, as was originally done in both of the Maryland properties illustrated on the following pages. Over time it was found to be more convenient to enclose the space between the main building and the kitchen. Even when this was done, however, provision was often made for a separate summer kitchen away from the house that could be used during the hottest months of the year. The dining room, on the other hand, was always a part of the formal main block. This room was given as much attention in its decoration as the parlor or drawing room in the typical Southern plantation home. In a rural society, entertainment centered to a great extent around the large dining room table.

Opposite page: *"Simple but elegant" is a phrase which can be used to describe many dining rooms of the old rural South. Furnishings are few, but are exceptionally well-crafted. At Joshua's Meadow in Maryland's Harford County, furniture of the Chippendale and Sheraton periods is handsomely arranged for formal dining. The estate once comprised several hundred acres conveyed in a grant from Lord Baltimore in the 18th century; the farm area has been reduced, but still occupies a sizeable portion of the rolling landscape.*

Right: *The original 1762 house, seen in the right background, is a perfectly symmetrical Georgian-style brick rectangle two stories high and one room deep. To the left foreground is the original story-and-a-half brick kitchen which was joined to the main house and converted into use as a living room in the 1930s. A new kitchen and bedroom wing was added to the main section at the same time.*

Below: *The dining room mantel is original, as are the doors to each side, the one to the left opening on a stairway to the second floor, and the other enclosing a storage closet. The walls and ceiling are painted white to reflect as much of the limited natural light as possible. This monochromatic scheme enhances the rich highlights of the mahogany Chippendale chairs and dining table and the Sheraton sideboard.*

*The high open cooking fireplace, with iron crane still in place, is the only artifact remaining from the old kitchen at Joshua's Meadow. At the time when this house was built, a kitchen fireplace was often left without an ornamental mantel. The handsomely beaded beams, however, indicate that the owner or his builder was not without a sense of decorative craftsmanship. The hearth is of brick made at the same time as that of the building, and the flooring is yellow pine.*

Opposite page: *An elegant manteled fireplace is the primary architectural feature of the dining room at Wye House on Maryland's Eastern Shore; the remaining woodwork is classically chaste in the early Federal style. A magnificent mahogany sideboard, thought to be the work of cabinetmaker John Shaw of Annapolis, combines Sheraton and Hepplewhite elements. Mounted on the corners are knife urns of the same wood.*

*Wye House typifies all that was gracious in the tidewater planter's way of life. The dining room lies at the back of the two-room deep, center-hall main house of the 1770s. To the right through the archway pocket sliding doors is the principal parlor or drawing room. The present owner of Wye House remembers midday dinner being served in this room in the early 1900s, her father and grandfather having returned from overseeing the work of fieldhands on some portion of the more than 1,000-acre farm. Following the multicourse meal, the gentlemen pushed back their chairs from the table and proceeded to nap, sitting upright, for exactly one hour before returning to the fields. That they should choose to relax in the dining room was by no means unusual; the practice of using this space as a sitting room had been common in many homes since the 18th century. The adjoining parlor was used in a similarly functional manner from time to time. If there were many guests present for dinner, the dining table was rotated and extended through the archway.*

# *The Mid-South*

Except for scattered French and Spanish settlement, the Mid-South was not widely populated until the first half of the 19th century. Within fifty years, however, there were businessmen in such centers as Memphis and Little Rock who had amassed considerable fortunes in lumber, cotton, or other commodities. These gentlemen built great homes, the Snowden house illustrated on pp. 56-58 being one of the finest in the Italian Villa style. In the last several decades of the century these men were joined by others of similar good fortune, the home of Henry Hanger, built in the 1870s and considerably enlarged in 1889, being typical of the Queen Anne style; its dining room is illustrated below. In rural areas of the Mid-South, the antebellum building tradition launched in the East earlier in the century continued to hold sway, but in the towns and cities stylish variations on Victorian architectural themes were most popular from the 1840s through the turn of the century. The Colonial Revival, a hybrid of Georgian, Federal, and late Victorian elements, was the last of the popular 19th-century Southern styles, the Tudor Revival never having found widespread acceptance as it did in Northern cities and suburbs.

*The Hanger family of Little Rock called its dining room a "saloon," a fancy term for a particularly decorative space where guests could be entertained in high style. All of the woodwork, including the pilasters and beams, is of oak. Less expensive cypress is found elsewhere in the house. The papers for the wall panels, cornice, and ceiling are typical of those used in the 1890s. The gas fixtures, original to the period, are once again operative. The sideboard and the fireplace, with its elaborate overmantel, provide handsome space for the display of family treasures.*

*Less than ten years after the Hanger house was extensively remodeled in the Queen Anne style, a very different kind of house was built just down the street in Little Rock. To be fashionably up to date in 1897 meant building in the Colonial Revival manner. The return to simplicity represented by the style is clearly revealed in the dining room. Small decorative touches, however, remained important, and these can be seen in the pine mantel and mirrored overmantel. The fireplace was built for a gas heater insert, and both the surround and the hearth are tiled, a common practice of the time. The lighting fixtures are fitted for both gas and electricity.*

Above and opposite page: *The exterior of the Snowden house in Memphis has remained virtually the same since its building in 1855, but individual rooms have changed somewhat, the dining room most of all. The transformation probably took place around 1905 when an enclosed side porch, the "Palm Room," was also added. "The dark dining room panelled with mahogany or hung with sombre leather," Edith Wharton wrote in* The Decoration of Houses *(1902), "is an invention of our own times." She preferred something lighter in spirit, a salle-de-manger in the style of Louis XVI, but most wealthy Americans ignored Mrs. Wharton's advice when redecorating. The popular taste was summed up in* House and Garden *in 1915: "An English Jacobean panelled dining room is always elegant."*

Overleaf: *The breakfast room of the Snowden house is as cheerful and charming as such a morning room should be. In 1915 the same* House and Garden *expert who recommended a paneled dining room admitted that it is "more suggestive of dinner than breakfast." The solution? "Fortunately, those who can afford such a room can afford also a breakfast-room, which provides the necessary sunshine and restfulness for the day's beginning." The features of this extraordinary room are captivating: the large windows hung with airy lace curtains; the painted paneled woodwork and the slender pier mirror; the bracketed marble serving shelf and the Italianate fireplace with pierced metal insert; and the tiered crystal chandelier.*

# *The Far West*

The "painted ladies" of late Victorian San Francisco architecture are unquestionably noteworthy. It is not the colors which intrigue us, however, as much as the features they emphasize, and because of San Francisco's unusual topography, these are many-layered and faceted. The extreme irregularity imposed by narrow and steep building sites is at an opposite pole from the symmetrical Colonial. Kitchens may have been built on one level and dining rooms on another; windows project at odd angles, casting interesting shadows on the outside and forming imaginative nooks inside. Because so much of old central San Francisco was destroyed in 1906, the unusual number of such buildings that survive are found beyond the downtown districts. Just as representative of Far Western building traditions during the Victorian period are the remaining Second Empire and Italianate style homes; two of the latter style are illustrated on pp. 62-65. These earlier homes were built on more accessible sites, and in floor plans closely approximating those found in homes in other regions.

*San Francisco's Noe Valley area was solidly built up in the 1890s and early 1900s with Queen Anne row houses. By the 1950s, many of these homes had fallen on bad times, but within ten to fifteen years almost all were reclaimed for new uses. The owners of one such building, the exterior of which is illustrated on the following page, found many distinctive ornamental features still in place, including the redwood wainscoting, fireplace, and plaster ceiling medallion of the dining room. Furniture appropriate to the turn of the century has been imaginatively used.*

*The row house was built in 1899 for a working-class couple that wanted to live as much as possible on one level; the residence might be termed a Queen Anne bungalow. The top floor has only recently been converted from a loft to a bedroom; the bottom floor serves as a storage area. The original kitchen, located just behind the dining room, was a pre-electric nightmare. It lacked both early charm and modern convenience. The modern modular arrangement works aesthetically because it makes generous use of oak and redwood.*

*The new kitchen of a second Noe Valley house dating from c. 1905 also makes use of redwood and oak, thereby repeating the use of such highly decorative materials in other rooms. Because the appointments are simple, they do not detract from the high-style craftsmanship displayed in the dining room. Although only five or six years separate the building of this house from the nearby residence illustrated on pp. 59-60, there was an evident turning away from the Queen Anne style to the Colonial Revival during the interval. All the woodwork was originally painted white, and a china cupboard was built into the wall. The cove ceiling contains decorative flourishes in the corners.*

*All that was left of the dining room in this San Francisco house before it was restored in the 1960s was its redwood wainscoting and simple soft pine floor. The residence, near the Mission district, was built in the late 1860s and always housed a middle-class family until bad times befell it during the Depression. Earlier, the house barely survived the earthquake and its fiery aftermath; the painted board and batten wainscoting was put up afterward, probably to cover over structural damage to the walls. The room has been left in its early 1900s form rather than being returned to the previous century. A table set with California Fiesta ware could not be more appropriate. The red shades of the handwrought iron chandelier and the modern stained-glass panels also help to brighten what could be a rather antiseptic setting, a look favored in the early 1900s.*

*The same kind of wainscoting also survived in the kitchen. A generous outlay of bright color has eliminated the "laboratory" appearance of many early 20th-century kitchens. Modern appliances have been carefully tucked into counters and cupboards. In redesigning the room, ample allowance was made for comfort and sociability.*

# 4.
# *Furnishings*

In the beginning, the kitchen was nearly an empty space. Only gradually over the years did it fill up with special types of furnishings and fixtures. The typical kitchen reached its most cluttered state in the early 1900s, and while the desire for time-saving gadgets had not been satisfied, planning for their use and accommodation improved greatly. In contrast, the composition of the average dining room has stayed much the same since the late 18th century. The standard pieces of furniture—a table and chairs, a cupboard or china closet, a serving table or sideboard—have changed only in design.

Furniture and other practical objects used in a kitchen or dining room may define the character of a room as much as its shelves and appliances. Many items—utensils and crockery, tables, chairs, mirrors and clocks, fixtures for hanging dish towels as well as pots and pans—are endowed with decorative as well as practical value. Kitchen antiques are collectible now for the reason that so many of them were crafted with care and an eye to their visual appeal. Objects used in the dining room are even more valuable; they were made as much for show as for utility.

Still, it is a mistake, contemporary nostalgia notwithstanding, to assume that everything about the antique past is worthy of artistic emulation. Take the lowly kitchen sink, for example. Despite the fact that the 19th century saw the introduction of handsome sinks constructed of slate and granite and even marble, the earliest kitchen sinks were purely utilitarian affairs, reflecting more the

Right and opposite page: *Close to Alamo Square, one of the few relatively level residential areas of the city, is a house built in the late 1860s. Like the other example from the same period, illustrated on pp. 62-63, little of value was to be found inside when restorers came to the rescue in recent years. The dining room contained only the original wainscoting. Now it is surely one of San Francisco's most handsome dining rooms. A marble fireplace suitable for a house of this age was put into place, as was the crystal chandelier. The special quality of the interior, however, comes from the artistry of a modern-day ceiling painter, Larry Boyce, who used old-fashioned methods and designs. The ceiling and cornice design is reminiscent of the work of decorator/painters of the 1880s and '90s who were enamored of naturalistic Japanese motifs.*

*Two views of the dining room at "Roseland," the 1846 Bowen House in Woodstock, Conn., display the practical and decorative furnishings typical of the early Victorian period. Two sideboards are used, one (above) which reflects the neoclassical Grecian style, and the other (below), the Gothic Revival. Displayed on the former piece is part of a Limoges porcelain dinner service.*

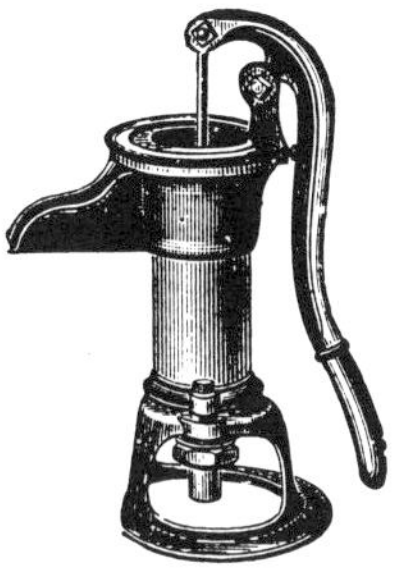

*A pitcher spout pump was often used in the kitchen for bringing up soft water from a cistern. The closed top prevented water from flowing out in all directions.*

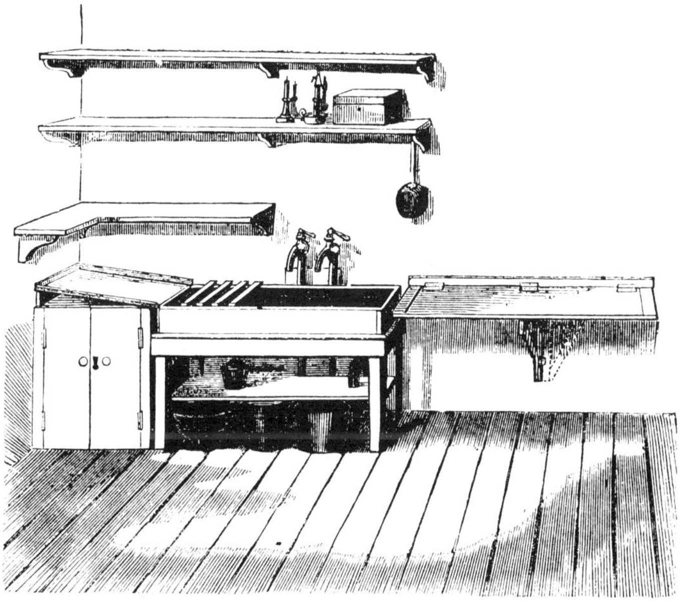

*The "housekeeping" editor of* The American Agriculturist, *a monthly newspaper for the farm family, offered this design for "a convenient kitchen sink" in 1865. It was made of wood and provided storage space at one side and in an open space underneath. The work shelf to the right folds against the wall when not in use.*

realities of such back-breaking chores as dishwashing and food preparation than the pleasures of aesthetic design. During the colonial period piped-in running water was virtually unknown, although sufficient water for washing dishes might be pumped from a nearby cistern. Most households made use of a portable supply—carried into the house by hand from the well. Any container large enough to wash in served as a sink. A bucket or basin might be set down on a worktable. During the 19th century the wooden dry sink came into use, and a washbasin was placed in its well.

The metal sink began to be widely used in the mid-19th century. In the country, water was often supplied from a cistern to a hand pump which was positioned at one side of the sink. Soft rain water was preferred for washing dishes, laundering, and bathing; well water was used for drinking and cooking. In urban areas, piped-in running water was brought to taps at the sink. The first metal sinks were of cast iron, in models either bolted to the wall or freestanding in the manner of a bathroom sink. It was considered unsanitary to enclose the drain pipe or to store cleaning supplies under the sink because of the accumulation of moisture there. Typical builder's specifications of the post-Civil War period would have read as follows: "Put up a cast-iron sink in the kitchen 18 x 36 x 6 inches, on cast-iron legs, supplied with both hot and cold water through 5/8 lead pipe, having over-flow, waste pipe, with trap and screw, &c., finished complete." The hot water source was probably a boiler which stood next to the cookstove. Although cast iron was the most common material for the sink, models were also available in soapstone, slate, and granite. By the early 1900s white enameled iron or steel sinks were widely in use.

Close to where dishes were washed was some sort of rack for towels. The roller towel—a continuous piece of cloth hanging from a roller—was the most distinctive 19th-century form. A folding wooden towel arm with three or more "fingers" was another common device. The most usual sight, however, was a line strung across the room to which both towels and rags were attached when drying or not in use.

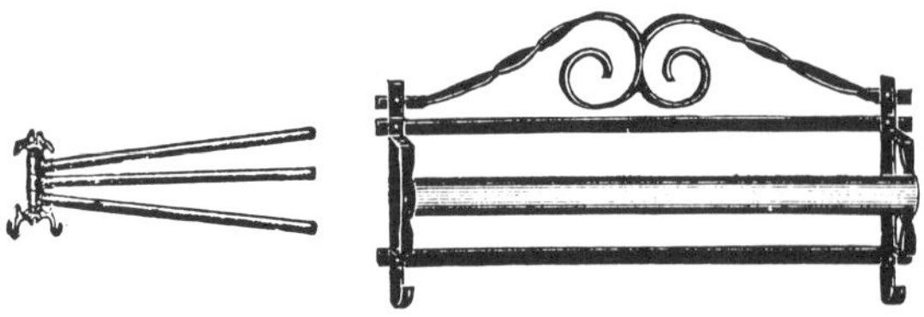

*Fixtures for towels and cloths were made of wood or metal and were designed to last for years. These were offered by Montgomery Ward in the 1890s.*

Nearly every kitchen, whether a separate room or not, was supplied with a worktable. In the earliest years this was likely to be a pine trestle table or an even more primitive appliance formed by laying boards across several barrels. The worktable was the place where food was prepared for cooking and most often the surface on which the family took at least two of its meals. The practice of covering the table with oilcloth became common in the 19th century; an odd piece of linoleum might have been used later. The housewife found it convenient to have a covering which could be washed easily and which would hide the effects of hard use. Not until the early 20th century were more sophisticated commercially-produced tables widely available to the housewife. These models often had enameled metal tops and were sold with a set of four matching chairs

*A pine trestle table is used today in the kitchen of the John Sydenham House dating from the early 1700s. Located in Newark, N.J., the house was meticulously restored in the 1950s, the fireplace mantel being added at that time. There had originally been a mantel and a panel reaching to the ceiling, but these elements were removed to make way for a coal range in the late 1800s.*

painted with white enamel. In most homes, however, the ordinary worktable continued to be one that was useless elsewhere in the house and had been relegated to the kitchen.

Seating furniture at first was very primitive, the usual colonial-period kitchen area probably containing nothing more than a few stools and perhaps a bench or high-back settee without cushioned seats. As long as the kitchen remained merely a work area in the larger "hall," its furnishings were portable pieces moved from one part of the room to another for different functions. When a separate kitchen was provided for, the room was furnished with castoffs from other rooms. Paintings and drawings of 19th-century kitchens show that the Windsor chair was frequently used. Miss Leslie probably had this type of chair in mind when she recommended in 1844 that the kitchen be supplied with half a dozen "common" ones. She also noted that two should be low models and suggested, as well, the use of two or three "wooden stools or crickets." Special provision for a work-weary wife or cook was roundly debated by the housekeeping experts of the time. Miss Leslie advised that "a cheap rocking chair would no doubt be considered a great comfort for the cook to rest in," but warned that it was to be used only "after she has done her work." By the late 19th century, however, the rocker was firmly established as a kitchen fixture to be enjoyed by any member of the family seeking the warmth of the cookstove. Both this piece and others used in the kitchen remained without upholstery or cushions.

The kitchen as a place of beauty and relaxation is a 20th-century invention. "Queen Anne in the front and Mary Ann in the back" is the way home economist Clara Laughlin described the manner in which the typical American home was furnished as late as 1912. For too long, she complained, "the largest outlay of money and taste was put into the 'front room' and the kitchen took the hindermost. . . ." A dazzling assemblage of gleaming copper and brass utensils, as can be seen today around many reconstructed "colonial" hearths, was unknown in most homes in either that period or later. Until at least the mid-19th century, most utensils were of the more common iron or tin. Sometimes they were hung from the wall on wrought- or cast-iron racks. Wood and pottery dishes and utensils were found in many homes well into the 1880s, as, of course, were those of pewter. Electroplated Britannia ware and silver-plated pieces began to replace pewter in the 1840s; aluminum, agate iron, and granite-ware utensils were introduced as substitutes for those of iron and earthenware in the late

*A drop-leaf table with four matching chairs was a fashionable purchase for a kitchen in the 1920s and '30s. This hardwood "breakfast set" was painted in an ivory enamel with dark blue trim and was offered by Sears, Roebuck in 1927 for $20.00. A few years later, in the Depression, the same set could be had for less than $5.00.*

*All American clockmakers made special models for the kitchen. This is a "kitchen oak" shelf model manufactured by E. Ingraham & Co., Bristol, Conn., c. 1895.*

Victorian period. More expensive materials such as porcelain, glass, and sterling silver were locked up in the dining room or pantry.

A mirror was sometimes hung on the wall of the Victorian kitchen or propped up on the mantel, although such a nicety was frowned upon by the experts on housekeeping. The punctilious Miss Leslie advised against it: "In houses where there is a kitchen looking-glass, hairs are frequently found in the dishes that come to table." The writers on cookery and housekeeping did recommend, however, the use of a reliable timepiece as the preparation of food was becoming more systematized. A clock became standard for the kitchen by the mid-1800s, and was usually a shelf model that could fit on the mantel or on a special wall bracket. The first mass-produced models for kitchen use were quite simple in design, a more ornate type being used in the parlor. By the late 19th century, manufacturers had created special oak models of considerable intricacy in mechanism and case; the walnut-cased variety, however, remained in the "front" of the house.

The flow of specialized devices for kitchen use increased without slackening from the early 1800s until well into the 20th century. Apple corers and parers, grinders, various choppers and slicers, different types of butter churns, coffee and spice mills, eggbeaters—all came in ever-improved models. The housewife, then as today, was interested in any gadget that would save time and energy. As the 19th century progressed, the shelves and work surfaces of the average kitchen grew more and more crowded. The development of the modern modular kitchen with ample built-in storage space in the early 1900s is striking proof that necessity is, indeed, the mother of invention.

The dining room, by contrast, has hardly evolved at all in its furnishing and layout. Writers throughout the 1800s recommended that it be equipped with three types of objects—a table, a set of chairs, and a sideboard, buffet, or serving table. A cupboard for the display and storage of china and other valuable possessions was considered a pleasant addition, but hardly a necessity. Since the room was often used but once a day, if then, and was designed with entertaining in mind, it is not surprising that its plan was kept simple. A table to accommodate a family and guests was sometimes about all that space would allow for.

In the 18th century two drop-leaf tables were used separately or hinged together for dining in homes that contained a formal dining room. The Sheraton double-pedestal table evolved from this form. Usually made of mahogany or cherry, it remains a handsome addition to any early period dining room. Various types of extension tables became popular by the mid-19th century and these, usually of oak or walnut, accommodated additional leaves. Some of the early ex-

tension tables were round with a heavy center base; later 19th-century models were often graceless blocks of oak with four stumpy legs and a center pillar. Such contraptions rarely won the praise of the decorators of the time. "I have never seen an extension table that was well-designed," Clarence Cook commented in *The House Beautiful* (1881), "though," he admitted, "they are often well enough contrived for their purpose." Cook and other critics were particularly vexed by the dark and heavy appearance of the furniture popular in the post-Civil War period. Not until the turn of the century did their preference for light colors and less ponderous furniture begin to be appreciated on the popular level. By that time, Colonial Revival designs in light oak and cherry for tables, sideboards, and china cabinets had become fashionable.

Above: *Whatever the period, the essential dining room furnishings remained much the same. Malbone House in Newport, R.I., dates from 1849 and was designed by Alexander Jackson Davis. The sideboard at right is in the Gothic Revival style; the console table at left and the table and chairs are earlier in style.* Below: *A.J. Downing recommended the use of an extension table for dining in* The Architecture of Country Houses *(first edition, 1850). When this model is closed, he explained, it "appears like an ordinary circular centre-table." A similar table is seen on p. 73.*

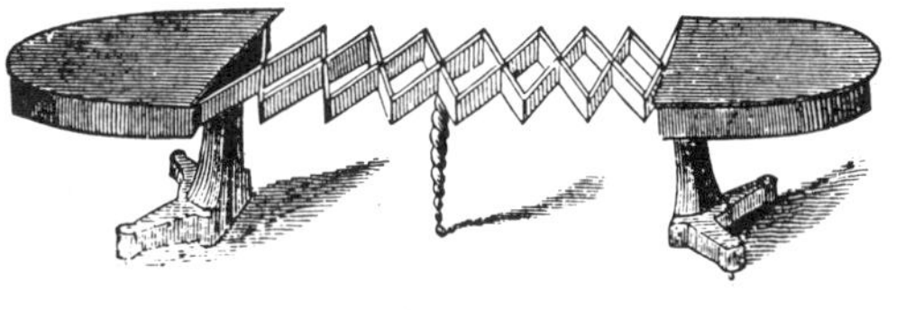

The dining room has always been a place to display family treasures, some of which may be used on the table. The built-in corner cupboard of the colonial period provided a handsome niche for Delft, creamware,

pewter, and silver. By the Federal period, a Sheraton-style sideboard was often used to display Chinese export porcelain, silver, and glass. Other portable furnishings such as the china cabinet, etagere, and what-not were introduced during the 1800s to hold objects worthy of the attention of guests. The elegant late-Victorian dining salon included a fireplace, the overmantel of which was composed of shelves for the display of knickknacks, and often built-in china cabinets and a buffet. Even in the crowded Victorian dining room, however, primary attention was given to the table and its setting.

Opposite page, top: *The dining room of the Christian Heurich mansion in Washington, D.C., built in 1892-94, is richly paneled with a coffered ceiling that repeats the design of the walls. The furnishings were designed for the room. Heurich, a successful brewer in the German tradition, displayed his wealth in a true old-world manner.* Opposite page, bottom: *The dining room of the Longworth family residence in Washington, D.C., as seen in 1905, was also monumental in proportions. Most of the furnishings, including the matching sideboards, are Victorian Jacobean. The dining table is of a simple type then coming into favor.*

Left: *During the mid- to late-Victorian period a sideboard was sometimes mounted with a great mirror in a carved wood frame. The mirror reflected the light from a chandelier and gave the room an extra sparkle and dimension. An etagere was usually mirrored, as well, with shelves extending from each side.* Below: *The furnishings of this dining room, photographed in 1911, reflect the popular turning back to "colonial" styles that had been underway since the 1890s. The dining table, chairs, and small corner serving table are in the new taste for the simple; the paneled sideboard with bracketed shelf and mirror is relatively uncomplicated. The plate rail with dentil molding is a handsome period touch.*

# 5.
# *Setting the Table*

A growing tendency to luxury in table furnishing runs side by side with increased elaborateness in cooking," housekeeping expert Christine Herrick wrote in 1888. She cautioned that, while "Both mark an advanced civilization and a healthy growth," they should not be "carried too far." The elaboration of the dining table was a trend that was well underway in the homes of upper-class Americans by the late 18th century. Following the Revolution, imports of fine china, glass, and silver from many parts of the world increased dramatically. One hundred years later, such furnishings were within the reach of the middle class as well, and the excesses of the rich were becoming a matter of controversy. The poor of the land knew nothing of luxury goods for dining, and, like the first settlers of the colonial period, they were much more concerned with putting bread on the table than in seeing to its proper setting.

A table set for dining was likely to be a very modest arrangement until at least the mid-1700s when individual sets of crockery came increasingly into use. At first, pewter, iron, and wood were staple materials for utensils and other dishes. Meals did not consist of many courses, but could be cooked in one or two pots. The vessels in which food was prepared were brought directly to the table and the contents not transferred to special serving dishes. Eating was a true communal experience, down to the use of shared spoons and knives which were dipped into common kettles and trenchers. In most households, forks were not standard equipment until well into the 18th century.

A place setting of glass, china, and silverplate, so familiar to us now, was unknown to the average colonist. Only gradually was the individual supplied with his own eating utensils and dishes. The adoption of personal place settings paralleled changes in the diet and in the preparation of food—from common one-dish meals to those of several courses, each requiring a special vessel. Pewter was used for many of these until the appearance of electroplated wares in the 1850s. Pottery was most commonly employed in place of china, and glasses for drinking were in short supply except in the best households until pressed pattern glass was produced in abundance in the 1870s and '80s.

The elaborate table decorations so often presented today as typically "colonial" were luxuries that few colonists could afford. The imitation of more advanced English social practices was the perquisite of the wealthy mercantile and landowning families. In the rarefied circles of the Anglo-American society of the late Georgian and Federal periods, considerable study was made of English and French dining practices and accessories. A "surtout-de-table" or centerpiece was considered basic for the table to display fruits and sweetmeats. The forerunner of the Victorian epergne, it was made of silver or porcelain in a pyramidal form and also held glasses for syllabub or jelly. Related in use to the centerpiece was the silver plateau which may have held the centerpiece as well as figurines and vases. George Washington ordered a mirrored silver platform from France which held a set of bisque figures and vases. Edward Lloyd IV of Maryland, proprietor of Wye House near Easton, illustrated on pp. 51-52, and the Chase-Lloyd House in Annapolis, proudly displayed a 29-inch-long silver plateau containing 29 porcelain figures in the latter house.

Dried flower arrangements were used on the table as often as natural bouquets. Wax fruits and flowers were also popular decora-

*The dining room of The Octagon, a Federal town house in Washington, D.C., designed by William Thornton for Col. John Tayloe in 1798-1800, is perfect in its period details. A silver plateau holds a centerpiece of wax fruit on a table formed by two drop-leaf tables. The home is now the headquarters of the American Institute of Architects.*

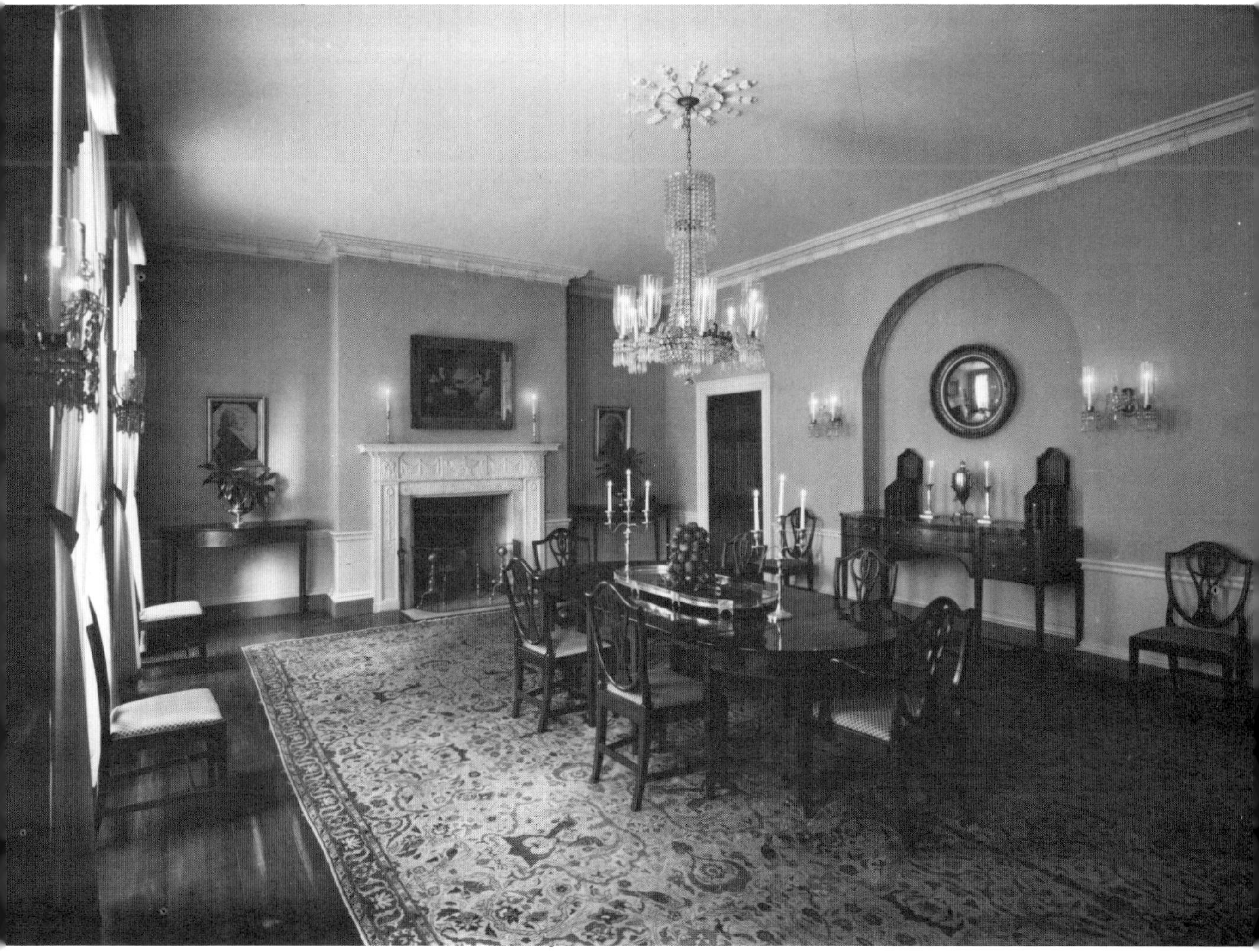

*Queen Anne chairs and a dining table were probably used during the 18th century in the Old Manse, Concord, Mass., built c. 1765 by the Rev. William Emerson. It is likely, too, that the smooth surface of the gate-leg table was left uncovered for dining during the early years of its use.*

tions, although they were more costly. Neither the dried nor artificial arrangements, however, needed replacing every week or even each month. Sugar ornaments were similarly useful, and often a large inverted cone cover in blue paper gave a pyramidal shape to a centerpiece. Because so many artificial materials were used as decorations, there was often a fixed, studied appearance to the table rather than the fresh, natural look popular in the Victorian era.

Before the early 1800s, special table coverings were known but limited in use, especially in the South. The kitchen table used for dining in the ordinary colonial home was often covered with a homespun cloth. The mahogany or black-walnut formal dining table found in more prosperous households was considered handsome enough to require only individual mats of straw or cloth. A linen runner may have been used in the table's center. Tablecloths of linen damask came into fashion in the early Victorian period and those of lace were a hallmark of late 19th-century elegance.

The proper setting of the Victorian table grew more complex each decade and was an exercise that required study and practice by the housewife. The number of manuals on such household tasks increased throughout the period; even the humble farmer's wife

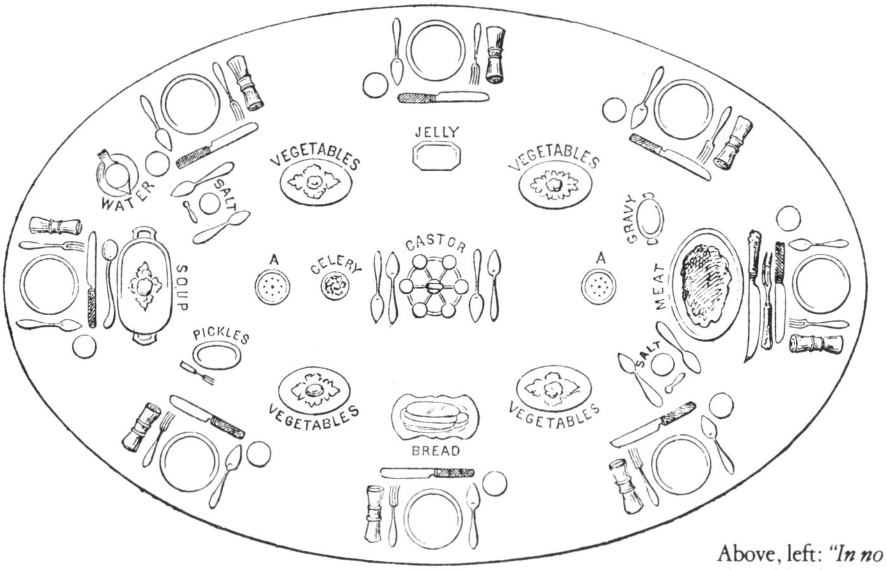

Fig. 1.—TWO-TINED FORK.

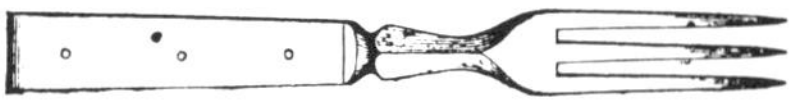
Fig. 2.—THREE-TINED FORK.

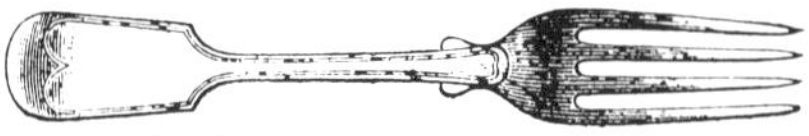
Fig. 3.—SILVER OR PLATED FORK.

Above, left: *"In no one thing in the household is order more desirable than in the arrangements of the table. . . ," a writer in the* American Agriculturist *explained in 1869. The diagram given is for a family of eight, and each member is supplied with his own knife, fork, spoon, napkin (with napkin ring), plate, and water glass. The head of the household served the meat, and his wife, the soup.* Above, right: *Use of the fork for eating was still unknown in many American households in 1869 when the household editor of the* American Agriculturist *provided instructions. "What we call 'society,' or 'good society,' has decided that the food should be conveyed to the mouth with the fork, and not by the knife." Fig. 3 is the model most recommended for use.* Below: *Napkin rings were a sensible feature when table linen was just that—linen and not paper. To supply each member of a family of five with a clean napkin at every meal would have brought the number needed, according to one housekeeping expert, to 105 per week. "There are few families, except among the wealthy, who own nine dozen napkins they can have in constant service."*

was instructed in table etiquette through columns in the agricultural papers. Each serving dish had its appointed place, as did the various pieces of a place setting for a typical three-course meal. Cruet stands, introduced in the late 18th century for condiments, were among the most important appurtenances. Commonly of Britannia metal or silverplate, these stands contained glass bottles for vinegar, ketchup, oil, bitters, etc., all of which, the arbiters of taste insisted, were to be filled daily. Other objects of common use at the time were napkin rings, knife rests, spoonholders, and castors.

Sets of china first became widely available in the early decades of the 1800s. Chinese export ware was a favorite among the well-to-do as had been Staffordshire creamware a generation or two earlier. Even the middle-income housewife could afford a "good" set of china for entertaining in the 1800s, perhaps a transfer-printed pattern from England or an American imitation. Following the Civil War, the average table became laden with products from the New Jersey and

21264
Price, 70c.

21265
Price, 85c

21270
Price, 88c.

21271
Price, 75c.

*Included in the 1895 Montgomery Ward catalogue were these typical china patterns: (left) Carnot Pattern Haviland, with pink and blue cornflowers and gold handles; (right) Yale Pattern Doulton, with blackberry blossoms and vines in a slate blue color and gold trimmings.*

Ohio potteries as well as finer wares from the Haviland district of France and the Staffordshire area of England. Mail-order houses such as Sears and Montgomery Ward regularly featured imported china in their catalogues of the 1880s and '90s.

Flowers continued to be an important feature of the well-laid table, but the emphasis was now on natural rather than artificial sprays. The Victorian epergne, often with a

*A silver epergne, decorated at the top with fruit rather than flowers, is the centerpiece used on the dining room table at the Mark Twain House, Hartford, Conn.*

trumpet-shaped vase at the top for flowers, could be a most imposing object. Although kerosene or gas lighting was likely to have been installed in the dining room during this period, candelabra and sticks were still recommended for use at the table. Those who possessed silver candleholders were reluctant to hide them away.

The degree of refinement reached in the 1880s and '90s dining room, the use of an immense variety of china dishes and silver-plated appurtenances, was not to be matched or outdone in the 20th century. The labor of

Above: *For families without appurtenances of silver,* The American Agriculturist *recommended use of a do-it-yourself table centerpiece. The stand is made of two tin plates with sockets and a glass rod or tube. Lilies of the valley are used with asparagus greens and ferns. "The idea of naturalness and grace," it was advised, "should pervade all arrangements of flowers for table decoration."* Below: *During the early 20th century, furniture in the late Jacobean style vied with the Colonial Revival for popularity in the dining room. Regardless of the style chosen, however, the table itself was more simply decorated than it had been in previous decades.*

*Since its construction in the 1760s, the John Ridout House in Annapolis, Md., has remained much the same in form and furnishing. The dining room might well have served as a model for those decorators and antiquarians in the early 20th century who sought a return to simple pre-Victorian elegance.*

keeping such pieces in a state of readiness, of setting and serving a table of great complexity, required the assistance of servants or, at least, daily household help. As domestic help became more and more difficult to obtain and expensive to keep, the many layers of Victorian table décor began to disappear. An elaborate flower-bedecked centerpiece might be replaced with a single posy in a crystal vase, the lace tablecloth laid away for use on only special occasions, the knife rests and napkin rings retired to a bureau drawer.

The return to simplicity at the table was widely applauded by fashionable writers such as Edith Wharton, Richardson Wright, and the new "domestic scientists." Each used the same adjectives—"uncluttered," "bright," "cheerful," "restful"—to describe the ideal new dining room. In style, such simplicity was a return to colonial Georgian and Federal-period fashions. In more practical terms, however, it meant that the housewife could begin to relax. With the preparation of food also being "modernized," few tears were shed over the loss of Victorian niceties.

# 6.
# *Decorating Styles*

The decoration of the kitchen has changed with almost every advance in domestic technology. The introduction of such innovations as running water, the cookstove, and gas and electric appliances usually resulted in changes to the room's basic layout, and, thus, to the way in which it was decorated. By contrast, the arrangement of the dining room has been effected only slightly by modern improvement. Two considerations, however, have often guided the decoration of both rooms that are closely related in the usual floor plan. The first and most important is that of cleanliness since the focus of activity in each room is food, its preparation and consumption. The second consideration, though more difficult to define, might be called warmth or charm. Despite the concern for sanitary conditions, some measure of homey domesticity—a wall plaque, a display of china, a decorative arrangement of pots and pans—has always crept into place.

The first kitchens were rather Spartan places, and it is unlikely that curtains were ever hung at the windows. The floor, generally of wood or brick, was usually left bare except for a sprinkling of sand, an early cleaning compound. By the end of the colonial period a wood floor might have been painted a solid color and given a spatter or stencil design. The fireplace wall was frequently paneled and painted; the remaining walls were simply whitewashed once a year. The display of utensils around the hearth, although less extensive than the mass of colonial iron usually presented today, was nonetheless visually interesting. Expensive pieces such as Delft plates are known to have been hung on the wall.

*The "hall" was one of two original first-floor rooms in the c. 1660 Stanley-Whitman House, Farmington, Conn., and provided space for cooking. The fireplace wall is sheathed in tongue and groove vertical white pine boards; the other walls are wainscoted with horizontal boards in the same manner.*

*The kitchen of "Roseland" in Woodstock, Conn., probably dates from the building of the house in 1846. The room is made up of appliances and decorative elements of various periods. Vertical wainscoting for walls was widely recommended in the mid-19th century; the linoleum flooring and the modern stove appear to be the most recent additions.*

The Victorian kitchen was a much more colorful room. It often included a cupboard, sometimes called a dresser, containing a family's everyday dishes and cutlery. Walls were sometimes wainscoted, and the surfaces above a chair molding were painted or kalsomined in neutral colors. Wallpaper was rarely used because it was difficult to keep clean. A plate shelf or hanging cupboard provided a place for odd pieces of china. The floor might be provided with rag rugs or carpet remnants, although oilcloth was widely used. "The best covering for a kitchen," Miss Leslie advised in 1844, "is a coarse, thick, unfigured oil-cloth, painted all over of one color (for instance, dark red, blue, or brown) and made to fit exactly." After the introduction of linoleum in the 1860s and '70s, oilcloth quickly faded from use except as a kitchen table covering. Fabric was used to brighten up the room—at the windows and perhaps as an edging on shelves. Pictures were few, perhaps a Currier and Ives print and a calendar with chromolithograph art.

The introduction of new appliances and gadgets caused the room to grow more and more crowded. A coal or wood stove was often four to five feet wide, and even taller if furnished with a high shelf; standing next to it might be a hot water heater. The average wooden icebox measured two to three feet across; an iron sink fitted with drying racks and a force pump to draw water from the cistern could take up nearly a whole wall. In 1879 one expert on "household management" commented, "The kitchen is a family laboratory, and a good cook should be a chemist." Considering the number of new devices which had to be fitted in and mastered, she also had to be a space planner as well as a mechanic.

The radical redesign of the kitchen in the early 20th century was inevitable. In the first wave of modernization, much that was only decorative was swept away. White ceramic tile often took the place of wainscoting; wall areas that were not tiled or fitted with cabinets were given a shiny coat of enameled paint, most often dead white. The same clean, enameled finish was applied to appliances, cabinets, and small utensils. As a writer in the *Encyclopaedia Britannica* ex-

*The Bureau of Home Economics of the U.S. Department of Agriculture disseminated much useful information for housewives in the 1920s and '30s. One series of pictures illustrated what were termed efficient "work centers" for the kitchen.* Top, left: *The "food preparation center" has as its base the sink and the cabinet to the right which held "dry" groceries and utensils for mixing and measuring.* Top, right: *The "cooking center" is the stove, in this case one fueled by oil.* Below, left: *The china cabinet or "closet" contained a pass-through so that dishes hot from the stove could be moved quickly to the dining room. The shelf made an ideal "serving center."* Below, right: *The sink serves as the "clearing away center" as well as the "food preparation center." A stool to sit on supposedly made dishwashing a less tiring task.*

*"Peasant style" was the term used in 1932 to describe the decor of this model kitchen in an Armstrong linoleum ad. Even the garbage pail is gaily decorated. All that is missing from the scene is a braided oval rug.*

plained in 1929: "The plan of the kitchen has come to depend on the relation, arrangement, and proportions of refrigerator, range, sink, and working-cabinet." Home economists made every attempt to systematize a housewife's kitchen duties and spoke of "work centers" for food preparation, cooking, serving, and "clearing-away."

By the late 1920s a reaction was setting in against this overly mechanical approach. The types of electric and gas appliances introduced during this period were smaller, easier to operate, and much simpler to keep clean than the coal or wood-burning equipment of the Victorian years. There was no reason why the room should not be more cheerful. Bright primary colors began to appear in place of white or light tones of gray and blue in walls and equipment. Washable papers in folksy patterns and prints became popular in the 1930s and continued in vogue until the '50s. Cotton hooked rugs of a vague "colonial" design were laid over linoleum before the sink and under the kitchen table. Canisters, odd pieces of china, copper and brass utensils, iron trivets, and salt and pepper sets were displayed on corner knickknack shelves and on the wall.

The dining room has always been the place to display one's finest possessions, some of which may be used at the table. From the 18th century until the present, it has been common to provide storage space for some of the best china, glass, and silver objects passed down over the generations. The first rooms set aside for dining in the 18th century were simpler in arrangement, however, than those of later years. In many instances, there were fewer treasures to display, and specialized pieces of furniture such as the sideboard and etagere, used for show as much as utility, were still novelties. In the early 1800s it became customary to place a sideboard in an arched wall recess. This practice not only reflected a fondness for neoclassical form, but served to center attention on such fine objects as candelabra, knife boxes, a tea set, and wine and liquor accessories.

Wall to wall carpeting became popular in the 1830s and '40s, and in some homes even the dining room acquired this type of floor covering. For reasons of cleanliness, however, a rug that could be easily taken up was usually employed. It needed only to be large enough to fit completely under the table and chairs. A crumb cloth or floor cloth was often

*The dining room of Oak Hill, built in 1801, is a classic example of Federal period design. Samuel McIntire is thought to have been the architect of this Essex County, Mass., home. The layout of the entire room is illustrated on p. 25.*

laid over the top of the rug or carpet to catch the overflow from the table. Rugs and carpeting, however, were never recommended for the kitchen because of the danger of grease stains and the retention of cooking odors.

Dining rooms grew darker and darker in color over the years. New forms of artificial lighting such as the kerosene hanging lamp and the gas chandelier made it possible to brighten the space more easily when required. The colors used in a candlelit Federal-style dining room of the early 1800s, for example, were often light shades of green and blue; the kerosene or gaslit salon of the 1880s might employ oak paneling and Japanese leather papers or Lincrusta-Walton. If these expensive materials were not available or affordable, similar effects might be obtained with paint, as for example: "a dado of rich maroon, with gilt figures, and a gilt and maroon molding in lines; above this, a very pale tint of olive-green with the cornice of maroon and gold."

Pleasant lighting for dining was of serious concern to the architectural critics of the late-Victorian period. Clarence Cook, author of the widely followed volume *The House Beautiful* (1881), complained: "It was a great deprivation when we were obliged to give up candles for illuminating. . . . I do not know why it was that when gas came into use it was

*Every square inch of space is covered with some decorative object or material in this 1890s dining room. A heavily embossed material is used as a wall covering to the level of a plate rail.*

The elaborately carved Renaissance Revival dining room set found in the Ronald-Brennan House (now the Filson Club), Louisville, Ky., possibly dates from the same time as the residence, around 1868. The room required little else in decoration. The chandelier was probably electrified in the early 1900s.

thought necessary to make all the chandeliers and branches clumsy and mechanical." Objection to gas fixtures which gave out a cheerful glow was, however, muted when electricity came into use ten to fifteen years later. Before the invention of the rheostat, it was impossible to control the level of lighting. Edith Wharton found the glare of bulbs offensive and suggested that they be provided with plain colored silk shades. A hanging lamp with a multicolored Tiffany-style shade, so properly admired today, was con-

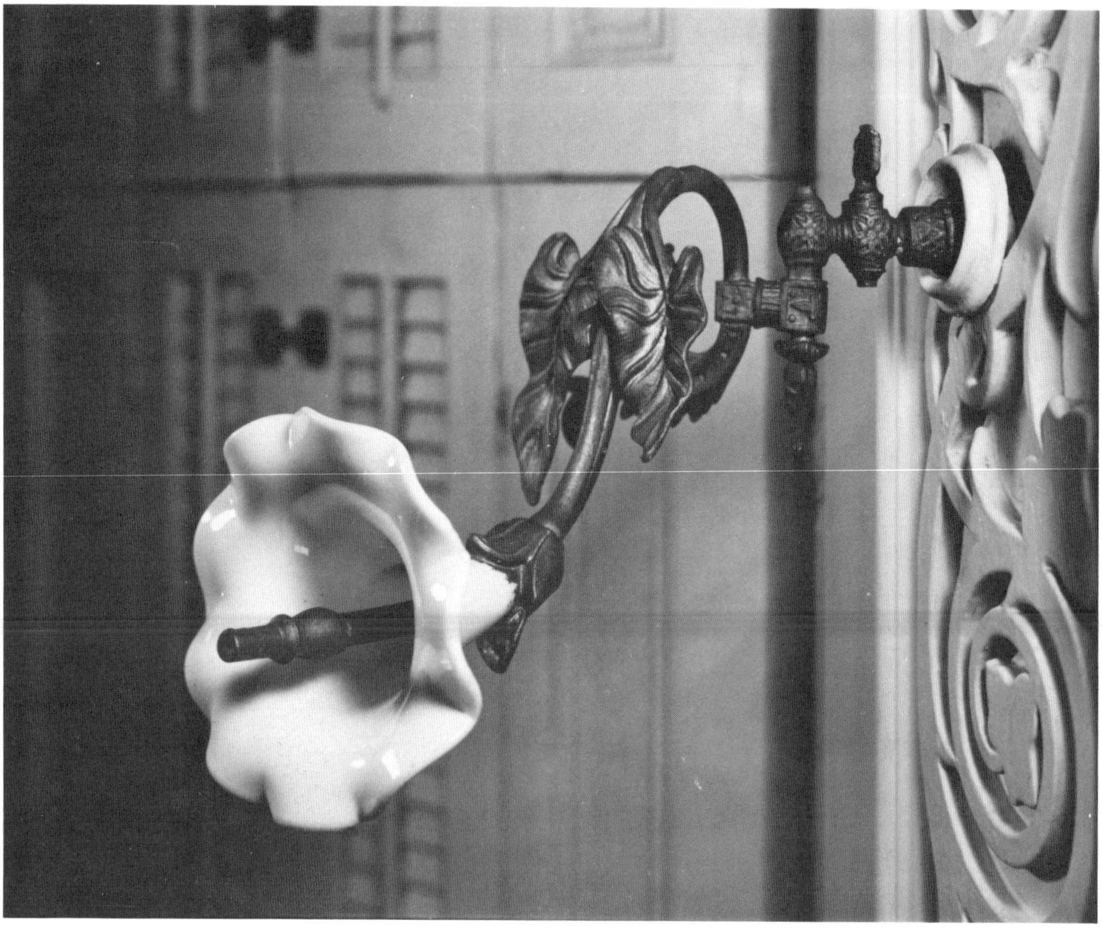

*This gas wall bracket, one of a pair found in the Ronald-Brennan House dining room, makes handsome use of a type of naturalistic design popular in the late 19th century.*

sidered particularly garish when illuminated by electricity, or so a *House and Garden* critic wrote in 1915. By the 1920s, all the high-fashion commentators agreed that dinner in the proper home should be candlelit, and it was not long before this fashion was followed in upper-middle-class homes.

Around the turn of the century the decoration of the dining room began to lighten. Heavy oak dining suites were no longer considered fashionable, and the over-laden china cabinet was ridiculed by the New York decorating establishment. Edith Wharton advised that a buffet or sideboard be placed in a recess, as it had been in the Federal dining room, and that the "ingeni-

ous but ugly extension table" be replaced with a graceful drop-leaf model. It had been a practice during the Victorian period to decorate the walls with pictures of fish and fowl, and nearly every writer on home décor advised their replacement with more soothing pastoral landscapes. The comments of one critic were typical: "It is not relishing to eat a delicate fish and look at a dead one hung upon the opposite panel; or, while enjoying a tit-bit of some rare bird, to see a whole string of them upon the walls." The most caustic words, however, were reserved for the display of sentimental plaques ("above all else avoid too many mottoes") and hand-painted china ("a little goes a long way").

*Chateau-sur-Mer, in Newport, R.I., is one of America's great Victorian mansions. Designed in the Italian Villa style by Seth Bradford in 1852, it was extensively enlarged and remodeled by Richard Morris Hunt in the 1870s along Second Empire lines.*

*The decor of the dining room of Chateau-sur-Mer dates from 1877-78 and was created by Luigi Frullini of Florence. Larger than life in all its intricately carved appointments of walnut, the room, nevertheless, was designed to be used on a daily basis. The table would seat at least twelve for dinner and more if extended further.*

Excesses of this kind seem less offensive today. The artifacts of the typical Victorian dining room and kitchen were laid aside so long ago that when they are rediscovered the reaction is likely to be one of appreciation. This recognition is similar to that accorded

antique objects of an earlier period by our parents and grandparents. If given a fitting place in the old house and not self-consciously displayed as mere curiosities, these decorative objects may add immeasurably to establishing the character of a period room.

*The detail of the overmantel carving also provides a close-up look at the tooled, gilded, and painted leather that is used as a wall covering; the same material covers the chairs and matching footstools. The motifs in the carving celebrate the bacchanalian joys of good wine and the good life as it was undoubtedly led at Chateau-sur-Mer.*

# *Illustration Credits*

In this list of illustration credits, sources not specifically identified in the captions are given. The following abbreviations are used to denote position on page: a (above), b (below), m (middle), c (center), t (top), bot (bottom), l (left), and r (right). Illustrations from the archives of the Historic American Buildings Survey are identified as HABS; those from the Library of Congress, LC.

*Cover/jacket:* Michael Kanouff (t-l), Allison Abraham (t-r), Eric Schweikardt (bot-r), Michael Kanouff (bot-l and c).

Pp. 2, 3, 5, HABS.

*Introduction:* p. 6, LC; p. 7, HABS, Stanley P. Mixon; p. 8, HABS; p. 9, HABS, Jack E. Boucher.

*Chapter 1:* p. 10, Private collection; p. 12 (t) LC, (b) *The Growth of Industrial Art (1892);* p. 13 (t-l, t-r, and b) HABS; p. 14 (t and b) HABS; p. 15, HABS; p. 17 (t) LC, and (b) Montgomery Ward & Co. catalogue (1895); p. 18 (t-l and t-r) New York Public Library Picture Collection, (b) HABS, Duane Garrett; p. 19 (b) LC; p. 20, LC; p. 22 (t) Private collection.

*Chapter 2:* p. 24, HABS; p. 25 (b) *Early American Rooms, 1650-1858,* Russell Hawes Kettell, ed.; p. 28 (t-l), Private collection, (t-r), LC, (b) HABS; p. 29, LC; p. 31 (a) LC, (b) Private collection.

*Chapter 3:* pp. 32, 33, 34, Eric Schweikardt; pp. 35, 36, 37, Bert Denker; p. 38 (t), Eric Schweikardt, (b) Linda Booth Schweikardt; pp. 39, 40, 41, Peter Ferencze; pp. 42, 43, Michael Kanouff; pp. 44, 45, 46, 47, Allison Abraham; pp. 48, 49, 50, 51, 52, Peter Ferencze; pp. 53, 54, 55, 56, 57, 58, Michael Kanouff; pp. 59, 60, 61, 62, 63, 64, Mark Gottlieb; p. 65, Tony de Guzman.

*Chapter 4:* pp. 66, HABS, Jack E. Boucher; p. 67 (t) Montgomery Ward & Co. catalogue (1895); p. 68 (b) HABS, Nick Aliferis; p. 70, William Penn Museum, Pennsylvania Historical and Museum Commission; p. 71 (t) HABS, Jack E. Boucher; p. 72 (t) HABS, Jack E. Boucher, (b) LC; p. 73 (t) HABS, (b) LC.

*Chapter 5:* p. 75, HABS, Jack E. Boucher; p. 76, HABS; p. 77 (b) Montgomery Ward & Co. catalogue (1895); p. 78 (b) HABS; p. 79 (b), LC; p. 80, HABS.

*Chapter 6:* p. 81, HABS; p. 82, HABS, Jack E. Boucher; p. 85, *Early American Rooms, 1650-1858,* Russell Hawes Kettell, ed.; p. 86, LC; p. 87-91, HABS, Jack E. Boucher.

# *Selected Bibliography*

Only those publications currently in print or readily available from public libraries are included in this listing. Many of the basic source books on American housekeeping and cooking technology have not been reprinted and remain inaccessible to the general reader.


Beecher, Catherine E. and Harriet Beecher Stowe. *The American Woman's Home.* Reprint of 1869 edition. Hartford, Conn.: Stowe-Day Foundation, 1975.

Benjamin, Asher. *The American Builder's Companion.* Reprint of 1827 edition. New York: Dover Publications, 1969.

Carson, Jane. *Colonial Virginia Cookery.* Williamsburg, Va.: Colonial Williamsburg, 1968.

Deetz, James. *In Small Things Forgotten, The Archaeology of Early American Life.* New York: Doubleday & Co., 1977.

Downing, A.J. *The Architecture of Country Houses.* Reprint of 1850 edition. New York: Dover Publications, 1969.

______. *Victorian Cottage Residences.* Reprint of 1873 edition. New York: Dover Publications, 1981.

Fowler, John and John Cornforth. *English Decoration in the 18th Century.* Princeton, N.J.: The Pyne Press, 1975.

Gould, Mary Earle. *The Early American House.* Reprint of 1949 edition. Rutland, Vt.: Charles E. Tuttle, 1965.

Handlin, David P. *The American Home, Architecture and Society, 1815-1915.* Boston: Little, Brown and Co., 1979.

Harrison, Molly. *The Kitchen in History.* New York: Routledge & Kegan Paul, 1972.

Isham, Norman M. and Albert E. Brown. *Early Connecticut Houses.* Reprint of 1900 edition. New York: Dover Publications, 1965.

Kettell, Russell Hawes, ed. *Early American Rooms, 1650-1858.* Reprint of 1936 edition. New York: Dover Publications, 1967.

Mayhew, Edgar deN. and Minor Myers, Jr. *A Documentary History of American Interiors, From the Colonial Era to 1915:* New York: Charles Scribner's Sons, 1980.

Peterson, Harold L. *American Interiors, From Colonial Times to the Late Victorians.* New York: Charles Scribner's Sons, 1971.

Seale, William. *Recreating the Historic House Interior.* Nashville, Tenn.: American Association for State and Local History, 1979.

Smith, Georgiana Reynolds. *Table Decoration, Yesterday, Today, and Tomorrow.* Rutland, Vt.: Charles E. Tuttle, 1968.

Stickley, Gustav. *Craftsman Homes, Architecture and Furnishings of the American Arts and Crafts Movement.* Reprint of the 1909 edition. New York: Dover Publications, 1979.

Stillinger, Elizabeth. *The Antiques Guide to Decorative Arts in America, 1600-1875.* New York: E.P. Dutton & Co., 1972.

Wharton, Edith and Ogden Codman, Jr. *The Decoration of Houses.* Reprint of 1902 edition. New York: W.W. Norton & Co., 1978.

# Index

*Since the terms "Colonial" and "Victorian" are far too broad to be anything but generally descriptive, they do not appear in this index. Consult the breakdown of the larger periods into component parts (i.e., Georgian, Gothic Revival, Italian Villa) under Architectural styles and Furniture styles.*